0248436303

ESSENTIALS OF ENGLISH GRAMMAR

ESSENTIALS OF ENGLISH GRAMMAR

D. Terence Langendoen

Graduate Center and Brooklyn College,
The City University of New York

HOLT, RINEHART AND WINSTON, INC.
New York, Chicago, San Francisco, Atlanta, Dallas,
Montreal, Toronto, London, Sydney

To David

PREFACE

This book is based primarily on material that I presented to high school English teachers participating in an eight-week NDEA Institute held at The Ohio State University during the summer of 1968. The limitations on the scope of this book are therefore explained in part by the limitations on what can be accomplished in thirty fifty-minute lectures, although considerable material that was not presented in those classes has been added. Like the course at the Institute, this book is designed to provide an appreciation of the structure and complexity of the English language, not a systematic description of that structure, or even of a small part of it. In addition, it is meant to provide an awareness of the various theoretical issues concerning the nature of language that are being debated among grammarians today. The study of grammar, and particularly the study of English grammar, is once again a vigorous and flourishing discipline on university campuses, and, for the first time, in governmental and industrial research centers. Not surprisingly, therefore, our understanding of language has been greatly widened and deepened of late, so much so that it is now being asked to what extent this new knowledge and understanding should be incorporated into primary and secondary school curricula, either to supplement or to replace the present English grammar curricula in the schools.

In fact, the effort to devise and to teach the "new English" curricula in the schools is already well underway. As can be imagined, the overall picture is both confused and confusing; textbooks and textbook series wholly dedicated to new approaches have been written and have been widely adopted. Traditional English grammar texts have been "updated" by the appendage of supplementary sections of more current vintage. NDEA Institutes, such as the one at which I taught, are being held across the country to acquaint English teachers with new approaches not only to grammar, but also to rhetoric and literary criticism. Naturally, there has been considerable objection to and criticism of these new approaches—both the material that has been worked into these texts and courses, and the way in which the "gospel" is being spread. The objections that have been made by linguists and serious English scholars generally have centered on the fact that, despite our collective advance in understanding, the gap between what we know about language and what remains to be learned has barely been narrowed. Moreover, there is little that can be called a "common body of knowledge" concerning the nature and structure of language. Even linguists who share a particular theoretical framework, or who work within similar frameworks, have profound disagreements over extremely fundamental issues; about all that can be agreed upon are the nature and the difficulty of the unsolved and open questions concerning language. Therefore, it may be claimed, we are in no position to make fundamental changes in the English grammar curriculum parallel to those that have been and are continuing to be made in the mathematical and physical sciences curricula. What can be, and what needs to be, changed are the attitudes of teachers (and of students) toward language and toward grammar. Teachers and students need to be made much more sensitive to the complexity and intricate beauty of English as a whole. They need to develop an appreciation of language akin to the appreciation of art and music that we expect any cultured person to develop. It is with this need in mind that the present book is being written.

The title of this book is the same as that used by two distinguished grammarians of the recent past, William Dwight Whitney and Otto Jespersen, for short introductions to English grammar. The three books are, however, very different from one another in content. Whitney's, written in 1877, is an old-style school grammar book designed mainly to inculcate the fundamentals of spelling, pronunciation, and style. Jespersen's, written in 1933, is a one-volume summary of his monumental seven-volume grammar of English, which manages to touch on just about every imaginable topic of English grammar. This book aims to be neither prescriptive nor comprehensive, but simply attempts to discuss some basic properties of English grammar in the light of recent developments in the theory of language. Certain sections of the book contain material that is more difficult or that is less directly related to the main purposes of the book. These sections are marked with a dagger (†) and may be omitted without loss of continuity. Finally, each chapter is followed by a set of problems and suggestions for further study. Again, the more difficult problems are indicated by a dagger.

I wish to recognize here a tremendous intellectual debt to my former colleague in the Department of Linguistics at Ohio State, Professor Charles J. Fillmore, whose ideas underlie much of the present work. To my linguistic mentors at M.I.T., particularly Professors Noam Chomsky, Morris Halle, and Jerrold J. Katz, I am indebted for many fundamental ideas and assumptions. Wayles Browne, Samuel R. Levin, George Miller, and Jay Keyser are to be thanked for supplying numerous helpful suggestions regarding many details of the presentation. Finally, I would like to thank Professor Wilfred Eberhart of the

College of Education, The Ohio State University, for administering a well-run Institute, and my wife, Sally, for taking the time to audit the course, and whose notes (not mine!) form the basis for this book.

New York City   D. T. L.
January 1970

CONTENTS

ESSENTIALS OF ENGLISH GRAMMAR

1 INTRODUCTION

1. The Goals of Linguistics

Grammarians make a distinction between universal grammar, the body of rules accounting for the properties that past and present languages of the world have in common, and the grammar of a particular language such as English. There are several possible ways of viewing the relationship between universal grammar and the grammars of particular languages. One is to consider universal grammar to be a sort of lowest common denominator of the world's grammars, with the grammar of a particular language consisting of universal grammar plus its own idiosyncratic rules that make the language it describes distinct from all other languages. Another way is to think of universal grammar as containing all possible rules for all possible languages, and to maintain that the grammar of a particular language is arrived at by eliminating all but a relative handful of the rules of universal grammar. At the moment, linguists have no empirical evidence that would

1

lead them to prefer one of these viewpoints over the other; the only bases we have at present from which to choose are taste and faith. However, one aspect of the relationship of universal to particular grammar does have a clear empirical basis: the human child uses universal grammar to arrive at the grammar of the language or languages in which he becomes fluent.

Many persons—linguists, psychologists, and philosophers among them—have expressed amazement and awe at the speed and accuracy with which children acquire fluency in the language of their parents and peers. Bertrand Russell has characterized the learning of language as the most outstanding intellectual achievement that most people ever make. Individual intelligence seems to have little to do with language acquisition except perhaps to speed it up or slow it down somewhat and to dictate in part the ultimate size of the vocabulary acquired. Eric Lenneberg, who has studied the relationship between language acquisition and measured IQ, observed that not until one reaches an IQ of around 40 or lower is language acquisition seriously retarded or prevented. Conversely, even the most intelligent of apes is completely incapable of ever acquiring the rudiments of language. Human beings are constructed to learn to speak and comprehend language, much as they are constructed to walk upright on two feet, and the conclusion we are entitled to draw from this observation is that, somehow, universal grammar is inherent in the human organism at birth.

To acquire fluency in a particular language, say English, a child has to be exposed to people who speak that language. Depending on the viewpoint one holds concerning the relationship of universal to particular grammar, one believes either that the child uses the bits and snatches of language that he encounters to form hypotheses about the idiosyncratic rules of English grammar, or that he uses this experience to reject those rules of universal grammar that do not seem necessary. In either case, the grammar that the child works at and refines from birth to six years becomes steadily more and more like the grammar of the language of his experience. This can perhaps be most easily appreciated by considering the child's progress in acquiring the sounds and rhythms of human speech.

Many infants, several months before they utter their first "word," make noises that we call babbling. Listening carefully to these noises, one finds that he can hear many of the sounds that go into the makeup of English words, and many of the rhythms and "melodies" characteristic of English sentences. But one can hear other sounds and rhythms too, sounds which are never part of English words and sentences, and some linguists claim to have encountered all possible speech sounds in the babbling of infants (which if true might lend support to the second of our two viewpoints concerning the relationship of universal to particular grammar). It is as if the child were tuning up his vocal apparatus in anticipation of his having to use it for speech, much as an orchestra gets ready for a concert. Later, once the child has begun to speak, he stops making those speech sounds which are not used in the formation of English words, and he even encounters some difficulties in making some that are used, notoriously the *r* sound in words like *red*. But unless there are physical deformities of the vocal tract or certain mental and emotional difficulties, the child eventually acquires an adultlike pronunciation of all the speech sounds and rhythms of English; at the same time, he loses the ability to acquire other languages without, at least initially, a noticeable accent.

The goal of the linguist is twofold: to arrive at a statement of the rules that form the basis of a person's ability to speak and comprehend a particular language, and, by the study of many languages and of the human organism itself, to arrive at a statement of the rules of universal grammar. (Over the years, linguists have developed various notational schemes for making these statements as precisely and concisely as possible; in this book we shall not be particularly concerned with formal notation, and shall be largely content with informal exposition. If, however, the reader learns or happens to know already one of these schemes, it should not be difficult to translate the informal statements in this book into formally expressed rules.) In most grammatical discussions, this one included, the goals have been made somewhat more modest: to arrive at a statement of the rules that are necessary for the explicit construction of sentences of a language, omitting the problem of formulating the rules for constructing larger linguistic entities, such as paragraphs or discourses, and omitting the problem of accounting for how people actually manage to use sentences appropriate to the situational context in which they are uttered. The reason for this is simply that the obstacles confronting anyone who even wants to make a start at tackling the latter two problems are so disproportionately immense at present that it is usually not thought to be worth the effort. The first problem, that of formulating the rules for the construction of sentences, at least has the virtue of being approachable.

The goal of the linguist can be paraphrased as making explicit what every fluent speaker of a language knows implicitly about that language. This suggests that the teacher of English grammar in the primary and secondary schools has, or should have, a parallel goal: much in the manner of Socrates in the dialogue *Meno*, making the student aware and appreciative of what he knows implicitly by virtue of his being a fluent speaker of his language. This contrasts sharply with the goal that many grade-school and high-school teachers of English hold: the implanting of a body of preselected rules that supposedly govern the structure of "correct" English sentences and connected prose. Part of the reason for this, no doubt, is the assumption many teachers have that their students do not know English and that it is their duty to teach it to them.

I do not mean to disparage this assumption, for it can be justified on several independent grounds. First, the language in which particular students are fluent may differ so substantially from standard English (a term that will be discussed below) that they need to be taught standard English as a second language, much in the way that modern foreign languages are taught. Second, the teacher may have no evidence that particular students, especially recalcitrant ones, are fluent in any language at all; such students use language fluently only with their peers and those adults that they do not perceive as authority figures, and typically a teacher is construed as one of the latter. Third, standard written English diverges considerably from even standard spoken English, so that students who are fluent speakers are not automatically able readers nor, more crucially, able writers. Moreover, standard English, particularly standard written English, is a somewhat artificial language when compared with true dialectal versions. The reason for this is that the standard language has come under conscious scrutiny and conscious manipulation by generations of critics, primarily teachers and professors of English but also journalists and other lay persons with the appropriate prestige and interest. To a considerable extent, therefore, the rules of grammar that govern standard English are arbitrary and conventional rather than natural; they must be taught outright, not by the mental midwifery of the Socratic tradition.

But even if we concede that there must be a certain amount of explicit teaching of the rules of standard English in the schools, the bulk of the time should be spent exploring the structure of the language in which the students are already fluent, in a way that will lead them to an appreciation of its nature and a consequent respect for its proper use in the communication of thoughts, ideas, and feelings. Almost all, if not all, the normative rules being explicitly taught today have to do with relatively superficial aspects of the language, the trimmings, and do not touch at all those aspects of grammar that have to do with the fundamentals of communication. But it is the latter that students should be continually made aware of.

Languages change over time, and not just trivially by the addition of some vocabulary items and the loss of others. The rules of grammar which govern the structure of sentences also change, most commonly by children arriving at grammars that differ ever so slightly from those of the previous generation. A standard language admits of change somewhat more grudgingly than nonstandard ones do, thanks to the conservative influence of tradition—that is to say, adults pass judgment on changes made, and children either ultimately learn to comply or stop trying to acquire the standard.

2. The Aims of This Book

In this book we shall be dealing primarily with contemporary standard American English, but we shall be examining its essential properties (as was indicated in the Preface) and not, except casually, the properties that depend upon the rules that are usually explicitly taught. Nor shall we pay attention to the fascinating and important topic of how this language has changed over the years. We begin by providing a few somewhat oversimplified definitions of theoretical concepts in linguistics, in order to guide our subsequent discussion.

By grammar, we mean the entire set of rules governing the properties of sentences in a language. It is generally agreed that there are three major aspects to the structure of sentences, so that grammar is conventionally subdivided into three components, one for each aspect. First, a sentence has a meaning, and the rules of grammar that govern the meaning of sentences are said to constitute the semantic component of the grammar (the Greek word *sēmantikos* means "significant"). Second, a sentence has a syntactic structure, which can be thought of as the parsing or diagramming of the elements contained in it. The rules of grammar that convert the representations of the meaning of sentences into their syntactic structures constitute the syntactic component of the grammar. Finally, a sentence has a phonological component, which consists of the rules that convert syntactic structures into speech.

In short, we say that a grammar has three components:

its semantics, syntax, and phonology, and their interrelationship can be diagrammed as in Figure 1.

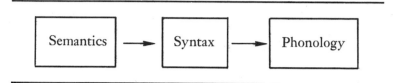

Figure 1. Interrelations among the components of a grammar.

In this book, we shall be concerned exclusively with semantics and syntax; this is a self-imposed limitation having to do with space, not because phonology is in any way less important or interesting than the other two branches of grammar. These same subdivisions are, of course, also appropriate for universal grammar.

In the course of our discussion, we shall have occasion to use certain technical terms. In particular, for the meaning of a sentence or discourse, we shall often speak of its deep structure; for the syntactic structure of a sentence or discourse, we shall use the expression surface structure. This use of these terms follows basically that of the contemporary linguist Noam Chomsky, whose work has made them quite well known and widely used.

To illustrate the structure and complexity of a few of the rules of English syntax, and of some of the artificiality and unnaturalness of a few of the normative rules of standard English syntax, I have devised a little game, called "The Walrus and the Alligator," which is modeled after a similar game, "The Old Woman and the Alligator," devised by Roger Brown with a similar purpose in mind. An account of Professor Brown's game can be found in an article by George Miller, "Psycholinguistic Approaches to the Study of Communication," in David L. Arm (ed.), *Journeys in Science.* Our game will be found in the next chapter.

SUGGESTIONS FOR FURTHER STUDY

1. For an important discussion of universal grammar and its relation to particular grammars, see Noam Chomsky, *Aspects of the Theory of Syntax*, Chapter 1. Also see Paul Postal, "The Method of Universal Grammar"; Emmon Bach and Robert Harms (eds.), *Universals in Linguistic Theory*.

2. The results of Lenneberg's research on the relationship of IQ to language acquisition are reported in his article, "A Biological Perspective of Language," in Eric Lenneberg (ed.), *New Directions in the Study of Language*. For a comprehensive survey and study of what is currently known about the biological bases of language, see Lenneberg, *The Biological Foundations of Language*.

3. Any similarity between the acquisition of language and the acquisition of the ability to walk was explicitly denied in one of the classical works of modern linguistics, Edward Sapir, *Language*, Chapter 1. Evaluate Sapir's arguments in

the light of Lenneberg's work and the discussion in this chapter.

4. Some of the most important recent research on the nature of language acquisition by children has been reported in Frank Smith and George Miller (eds.), *The Genesis of Language*, and in Thomas G. Bever and William Weksel (eds.), *The Structure and Psychology of Language*. Also see John Lyons and R. J. Wales (eds.), *Psycholinguistics Papers*; Leon A. Jakobovits and Murray S. Miron, *Readings in the Psychology of Language*.

5. For some views by linguists on the teaching of language, particularly grammar, in the schools, see J. Emig, J. Fleming, and H. Popp (eds.), *Language and Learning*. The essays by Dwight Bolinger, H. A. Gleason, Jr., Martin Joos, and Peter S. Rosenbaum are particularly recommended. See also Neil Postman and Charles Weingartner, *Linguistics: A Revolution in Teaching*; H. A. Gleason, Jr., *Linguistics and English Grammar*.

6. The classic introduction to grammar, in the three-fold sense described here, and to the study of language change, is Leonard Bloomfield, *Language*. No subsequent introduction to the subject matter of linguistics has even come close to replacing it, although an excellent introductory work has just appeared, John Lyons, *Introduction to Theoretical Linguistics*. Other recent introductory works, less comprehensive, include Dwight Bolinger, *Aspects of Language*; Ronald Langacker, *Language and its Structure*; D. Terence Langendoen, *The Study of Syntax*; Peter Rosenbaum and Roderick Jacobs, *English Transformational Grammar*.

7. The most comprehensive treatment of English phonology to date is to be found in Noam Chomsky and Morris Halle, *The Sound Pattern of English*. For phonology in general, see Robert Harms, *Introduction to Phonological Theory*.

2

"THE WALRUS AND THE ALLIGATOR"

"The Walrus and the Alligator" is played by two persons. "Walrus" is to say any declarative sentence he pleases, and "Alligator" must respond in a particular way to each sentence that Walrus says. To show how the game is played, I provide here a few illustrative sets of statements by Walrus and replies by Alligator.

1. WALRUS: I like ice cream.
   ALLIGATOR: Don't I?

2. w: You don't seem to understand me.
   A: Do you?

3. w: Your father can do a hundred push-ups.
   A: Can't he?

4. w: Louise is intelligent.
   A: Isn't she?

5. w: We won't tolerate such nonsense.
   A: Will we?

Most of you who have studied English grammar will no doubt have recognized that Alligator's task is to provide the "tag question" appropriate to Walrus's statement as if he were Walrus himself, and all of you who are fluent speakers of English will likely have no difficulty at all in playing the part of Alligator. For example, if Walrus were to say to you:

6. w: The sky looks threatening.

I am certain that you would unhesitatingly reply:

A: Doesn't it?

The question that I should now like to pose is, How much English grammar does one have to know in order to play the part of Alligator? The answer is, Quite a bit. In particular, Alligator must obey the following rules:

a. He must determine the person, number, and gender of the subject of Walrus's statement, and then select the appropriate personal pronoun. This is easy in statements 1, 2, and 5, since the subject of the statement is already a personal pronoun; the task is a little trickier in 3, 4, and 6. Alligator must recognize that *father* designates a male, that *Louise* is used of females, that *sky* is neuter, and that each of these is third person singular.

b. Alligator must determine whether Walrus's statement contains a so-called helping verb. If it does, then his reply makes use of the same helping verb, as in 2 through 5; if not, he must use the form of the verb *do* which is the same in tense and number as the main verb in Walrus's statement, as in 1 and 6.

c. He must figure out whether Walrus's statement is positive or negative; his reply will be the opposite. If the reply is negative, then the contracted form of the negative word, *n't*, is attached to the helping verb or form of *do*.

d. The elements of Alligator's reply must appear in this order: first, helping verb or form of the verb *do*; second, *n't*, if any, attached to that verb; third, subject pronoun. In other words, the helping verb and subject pronoun are "inverted."

It is a worthwhile conceptual exercise for this day and age to consider the problem of instructing a computer to play the role of Alligator. Those of you who are familiar with the current state of the art of computer programming undoubtedly know what a difficult problem this would be, especially when you realize that the task is to respond to *any* declarative sentence in English. Humans have very little difficulty—but that they may have some difficulty with particular statements by Walrus will now be shown.

As a homework exercise, I gave my forty-six students, all of whom were junior high school and high school teachers of English,[1] a set of ninety-one statements uttered by a hypothetical Walrus. The first five of these had correct Alligator replies, as in examples 1 through 6 in this chapter. The students were asked to play Alligator for the remaining eighty-six examples, and to write their replies directly below each statement. I should now like to discuss some of the more interesting of these Walrus-Alligator exchanges (at this point I should like to express my gratitude to my assistant, William Roberts, and to his wife, for making the tabulation).

The first interesting collection of examples has to do with the use of the verb *have*. Consider the following:

7. w: I have to go home now.
   A: Don't I?   36 replies
      Haven't I?   9 replies
      Do I?   1 reply

---

[1] Their geographical distribution was as follows: thirty lived in Ohio (eight in greater Columbus), four were from Illinois, two from New York, and one each from Wisconsin, Michigan, Pennsylvania, New Jersey, Massachusetts, North Carolina, Georgia, Florida, Arizona, and California.

8. w: I've been waiting a long time.
   A: Haven't I?   45
      Have I?   1
9. w: I have five cents in my pocket.
   A: Haven't I?   26
      Don't I?   20
10. w: I've got five cents in my pocket.
    A: Haven't I?   35
       Don't I?   8
       Have I not?   1
       Have I?   1
       no reply   1
11. w: I haven't got five cents to my name.
    A: Have I?   38
       Do I?   6
       Haven't I?   2
12. w: I have not five cents to my name.
    A: Have I?   29
       Do I?   17

Quite clearly, the group seems to have been divided on whether or not, in certain constructions, the verb *have* is a helping verb. From example 8 it is clear that, when used to indicate perfect aspect, *have* is universally considered a helping verb (one person seems to have got part *c* of the rule, the part involving negation, wrong in examples 7, 8, and 10, and two people got it wrong in 11, but we shall disregard this). From examples 9 and 12, we see that opinion is most sharply divided when *have* is used alone to indicate possession. By a relatively small majority, *have* is taken to be a helping verb in these cases, although I have a feeling that these results are like having only the upstate New York vote count—once the New York City count is in, the swing would be to the other side (my own Alligator response would be "Don't I?" to example 9 and "Do I?" to 12). When *have* is used together with *got* in Walrus's statement to indicate possession, then the swing is very sharply toward considering *have* a helping verb, although a minority held out for the other view even here. On the other hand, the *have* of *have to*, meaning *must*, is overwhelmingly (by a four-to-one margin) considered not to be a helping verb. The one person who refused to give a reply to example 10 felt that 10 wasn't good English and therefore shouldn't be dignified by a reply (although he or she did, apparently, reply to 11).

On the basis of these results, I think it is fair to conclude that the standard English treatment of *have* is not fixed, and that although there are clear preferences for treating it as a helping verb in certain constructions and not in others, the minority views, wherever they exist, cannot be regarded as nonstandard.

The next set of examples has to do with the expletive *there*.

13. w: There's a book on the table.
    a: Isn't there?   44
       Isn't it?   1
       Is there?   1

14. w: There isn't any chalk on the rack.
    a: Is there?   46

15. w: There is no chalk on the rack.
    a: Is there?   45
       Isn't there?   1

16. w: There happen to be six books on the table.
    a: Aren't there?   26
       Don't there?   18
       Don't they?   2

From all these examples, we see that for purposes of Alligator's response, *there* is taken to be the subject of Walrus's statement, even though the "logical subjects" of those sentences are different (although one person responded to the logical subject of 13 and two persons to that of 16). The responses to 16 are particularly interesting; they indicate that a majority disregarded entirely the verb *happen* (but *not* its tense and number), and responded with the present plural form of *be*! The logic of this decision, in any event, is clear; since *happen* does not materially contribute to the meaning of 16, the sentence might just as well have been "There are six books on the table," to which Alligator's reply would necessarily be "Aren't there?" A considerable minority, nevertheless, did follow the usual rules in forming their responses. Next we consider some examples with a variety of helping verbs.

17. w: I must go home now.
    A: Mustn't I?   42
       Don't I?   2
       Must I not?   1
       Won't I?   1

18. w: I may not see you tomorrow.
    A: May I?   32
       Will I?   13
       Won't I?   1

19. w: I may see you tomorrow.
    A: Won't I?   17
       May I not?   11
       Mayn't I?   10
       Might I?   3
       Mightn't I?   2
       Can't I?   1
       Shall I?   1
       Will I?   1

20. w: You ought not smoke.
    A: Ought you?   35
       Should you?   9
       Had you?   1
       Shouldn't you?   1

21. w: You ought to smoke.
    A: Oughtn't you?   26

Shouldn't you?   19
Hadn't you?   1

I must confess that I hadn't expected the large number of different responses to these statements, particularly to 19, which set a record of eight different replies. The bewildering array in 19 is probably due in part to a feeling of dislike for the expression "Mayn't I?" which is called for by the rules and which ten persons did use. The most conservative way out is to reply "May I not?" a response that eleven settled upon (note that when *not* is not contracted, it is not inverted along with the verb but remains after the subject pronoun). A plurality, but not a majority, had a different solution: they found a helping verb similar in meaning to *may*, but whose negative form did not strike them as sounding odd. Seventeen chose *will*, two *might*, and one *can*. The reason *will* was chosen most frequently is that the meaning of Walrus's statement is equivalent to "It may be that I will see you tomorrow." Finally, five persons broke the rule regarding negativity and answered without using *not*, or *n't*, but, significantly, they also chose different helping verbs— three opted for *might*, one for *shall*, and another for *will*.

The responses to sentence 21, though less spectacular, can be similarly explained. A significant minority were not content with the expression *oughtn't*; nineteen substituted for it *shouldn't*, and one *hadn't*. The few deviant responses to 17 indicate that just a handful of persons did not care for *mustn't*; a different helping verb was chosen by three persons, and one used the locution "Must I not?" Finally, the responses to 18 and 20 indicated some dissatisfaction with the use of affirmative *may* and *ought* in reply to Walrus sentences in which these occurred with the negative. *Will* was used for *may* by fourteen persons (one of whom violated the rule regarding negativity); ten used *should* for *ought* (again with one person using the negative); and one used *had*.

The next two examples set a trap.

22. w: I'm not going to the store now.
    A: Am I?   46
23. w: I'm going to the store now.
    A: Aren't I?   28
       Am I not?   17
       Ain't I?   1

As any good dictionary will tell you, *ain't* was formerly the standard contracted form of *am not*; however, its later use in place of *isn't*, *aren't*, *hasn't*, and *haven't* led to its elimination from standard English, with the result that there is at present no totally acceptable standard contraction of *am not*. As the response to sentence 23 shows, *aren't* is now used with a first person singular subject by a majority of speakers of standard English.

The next set has to do with negativity.

24. w: The boy never watched his sister.
    A: Did he?   46
25. w: The boy watched his sister at no time.
    A: Did he?   38
       Didn't he?   8
26. w: The boy rarely watched his sister.
    A: Did he?   41
       Didn't he?   5
27. w: The boy watched his sister infrequently.
    A: Didn't he?   43
       Did he?   3
28. w: The boy often watched his sister.
    A: Didn't he?   46
29. w: The boy watched no one.
    A: Did he?   36
       Didn't he?   10
30. w: No one watched my sister.
    A: Did he?   23
       Did they?   17

> Didn't they?   4
>
> Didn't he?   2
>
> 31. w: No one watches TV any more.
>
>   A: Do they?   26
>
>   Does he?   17
>
>   Don't they?   2
>
>   Doesn't he?   1

These results indicate that there were some differences in the criteria used to judge the negativity of Walrus's statements. From example 24 we learn that *never*, just like *not*, necessarily makes negative the statement it occurs in; from 28 we see, not surprisingly, that *often* keeps its statement affirmative. Differences arose over the interpretation of sentences containing *at no time*, *rarely*, and *infrequently*. A very considerable majority judged sentences with *at no time* and *rarely* in them negative, whereas the sentence with *infrequently* was judged positive. A minority in each case, however, held out for the opposite opinion. (We could, I suppose, take the point of view that they simply made mistakes, and that if they had a chance to do the exercise over again, they would agree with the majority opinion. But this is not supported by the comments that these teachers wrote in the margin, nor by their general discussion with me in class. By and large, they stood quite vigorously by their responses as Alligator.)

Example 29, in which a negative direct object occurs, was judged negative by roughly a four-to-one margin, and 30 and 31, with negative subjects, were judged negative by somewhat wider margins. The latter two examples are interesting in another respect, because they show a splitting of opinion regarding the number of the expression *no one*. In example 30, twenty-three persons took it to be singular, and twenty-three others took it to be plural—an even split. In 31, eighteen persons decided it should be singular and twenty-eight plural. That more persons took it to be plural in 31 than in 30 is especially surprising, since in 31 the verb in Walrus's statement agrees in number with the subject *no one* and is singular, whereas the verb shows no agreement at all in 30! It is in these cases, and the cases illustrated by the next group of examples, that a conflict between the normative grammar for standard English and the internalized grammar that most people acquire outside of school arises with special force. Normative grammar dictates that the expressions *no one* and *everyone* are always referred to by a singular pronoun, such as *he*, and that if used as a subject, the verb agrees with it as a singular. Most people also internalize the second part of this, but by and large they acquire naturally a grammar in which the pronoun that refers to these expressions is in many cases a plural one, such as *they*. My English-teacher students were in a bind as Alligators in this exercise, and it is not surprising that the responses were as divided as they were. The next group of examples continues this theme.

32. w: Everyone likes me.
    a: Don't they?   34
       Doesn't he?   12

33. w: Everyone likes one another here.
    a: Don't they?   34
       Doesn't he?   10
       Do they?   1
       Does he?   1

34. w: All the students like one another here.
    a: Don't they?   46

35. w: Everyone likes himself here.
    a: Doesn't he?   45
       Don't they?   1

36. w: Everyone likes everyone here.
    a: Don't they?   31
       Doesn't he?   14
       Doesn't she? 1

37. w: Not everyone likes himself here.
    a: Does he?   43
       Doesn't he?   3

38. w: Not everyone likes everyone else here.
       a: Do they?   34
           Does he?   12
39. w: Few people like me.
       a: Do they?   39
           Don't they?   7
40. w: A few people like me.
       a: Don't they?   46
41. w: Seldom did anyone say anything.
       a: Did they?   22
           Did he?   19
           Didn't he?   3
           Didn't they? 2

From examples 32, 33, 36, and 38 on the one hand, and 35 and 37 on the other, we find that when *everyone* is treated semantically as a collective expression, about 70 percent of the respondents refer to it with the plural pronoun, and that when it is treated as a singular, nearly 100 percent refer to it with the singular pronoun (there was one holdout for a plural *they* in response to 35). The *anyone* of 41 is treated just as the *no one* of 30—half use the singular pronoun for it, and half the plural. As would be expected, the subject quantified by *all* was considered plural by everyone.

A very small minority treated 37, with a negative subject, as a positive sentence, but for some reason no one did this to 38. The presence of *seldom* in 41 was handled just as that of *rarely* in 26, all but five considering the resulting sentence negative. Finally, examples 39 and 40 illustrate the tendency to take the quantifier *few* as negative in force, but to take *a few* as positive.

The next examples have to do with the problem of identifying the subject of a sentence containing a parenthetical expression.

42. w: I believe that Dr. Spock is innocent.
       a: Don't I?   36
           Isn't he? 10

43. w: Dr. Spock, I believe, is innocent.
    a: Isn't he?   43
       Don't I?   3

44. w: Dr. Spock is innocent, I believe.
    a: Isn't he?   38
       Don't I?   7
       Isn't it?   1

45. w: I don't think that Dr. Spock is innocent.
    a: Do I?   37
       Is he?   8
       Don't I?   1

46. w: Dr. Spock, I don't think, is innocent.
    a: Is he?   34
       Isn't he?   9
       *Do he?[2]   2
       Do I?   1

If we examine 42 and 45, we observe that only four-fifths of the respondents consider *I* to be the real subject and *think* the real verb of sentences that start off with *I think* and *I don't think*; the remaining one-fifth or so hold that the subject and verb of the subordinate clause are the real subject and verb in these sentences. The negativity of the sentence as a whole, however, is determined by the presence or absence of a negative with the verb *think*, as example 45 shows. We call the expression *I think* a parenthetical expression, since as far as its form goes, it is inserted at various points in a sentence without being closely connected with any one part of the sentence; compare 43, 44, and "Dr. Spock is, I think, innocent." In these sentences, *Dr. Spock*, and not *I*, is considered the subject by a considerable majority, but there are a few holdouts for *I*. The same is true for 46; two persons gave the aberrant response "Do he?" to protest, I think, what they consider to be an ungrammatical statement on

---

[2] An asterisk preceding an expression indicates that the expression is ungrammatical.

Walrus's part (I sympathize; 46 doesn't strike me either as particularly good English).

The next collection has to do with the problem of determining the gender of the subject.

47. w: One of my friends is coming.
    A: Isn't he?   37
       Isn't she?   9

48. w: The child is crying.
    A: Isn't he?   31
       Isn't it?   13
       Isn't she?   2

49. w: The baby is crying.
    A: Isn't he?   30
       Isn't it?   16

50. w: The boat is sinking.
    A: Isn't it?   45
       Isn't she?   1

51. w: The *Queen Mary* has made her last voyage.
    A: Hasn't she?   41
       Hasn't it?   5

52. w: The *Queen Mary* has been scrapped.
    A: Hasn't she?   30
       Hasn't it?   16

53. w: My cousin is handsome.
    A: Isn't he?   46

54. w: My cousin is pretty.
    A: Isn't she?   46

55. w: My cousin speaks Chinese fluently.
    A: Doesn't he?   46

56. w: My cousin married a son of a millionaire.
    A: Didn't she?   46

57. w: My uncle's spouse won't eat caviar.
    A: Will she?   44
       Won't she?   2

58. w: My father's only child is brilliant.
       A: Isn't he?   25
           Isn't she?   17
           Aren't I?   2
           Am I not?   2

If one does not know the gender of a person referred to by a noun, he will generally use a masculine pronoun, such as *he*, to refer to him. Thus, in example 55, in which Alligator has no information about the gender of Walrus's cousin, everyone used *he* to refer to him. That nine persons used the feminine pronoun in response to 47 is explained by the fact that in doing this exercise the students pretended they were Walrus as well as Alligator; those nine presumably feel that they have only female friends. Examples 48 and 49 illustrate the possibility of using the neuter pronoun to refer to a young human whose gender is not known, but it will be noted that the respondents preferred the use of a non-neuter pronoun by a two-to-one margin. Conversely, we can use the feminine pronoun to refer to ships, as is illustrated by 50–52, but as 50 shows, all but one of the respondents must be landlubbers. Even though a feminine pronoun was used in Walrus's statement 51 to refer to the *Queen Mary*, five persons used *it* in their response. In the absence of such a pronoun in Walrus's statement 52, one-third of the group used the neuter pronoun.

The respondents were able to use indirect evidence about the gender of the subjects of Walrus's statements in examples 53, 54, 56, and 57. Since the adjective *handsome* is typically only predicated of males and *pretty* of females, everyone used *he* in 53 and *she* in 54. In 56, they used the information that the subject had a male spouse and therefore must be a woman; similarly in 57. In order to interpret the results of 58, which are very interesting, I must point out that the class was made up of thirty-two women and fourteen men. Apparently, about half of the women must have calculated who the expression *my father's only child* necessarily refers to and, identifying with Walrus, used *she* in their response. Four persons went so far as to use the first person subject in their reply, which I think is surprising.

The next set of examples has to do with *either . . . or* and *neither . . . nor* subjects.

59. w: Either the fellows or the girls will stay.
    A: Won't they?   46

60. w: Either John or Tom will stay.
    A: Won't he?   40
       Won't they?   6

61. w: Either John or Sue will stay.
    A: Won't they?   22
       Won't she?   19
       Won't he?   3
       Won't he or she?   1
       no reply   1

62. w: Either Sue or John will stay.
    A: Won't he?   23
       Won't they?   20
       Won't she?   1
       Won't she or he?   1
       no reply   1

63. w: Either Sue or the boys will stay.
    A: Won't they?   46

64. w: Either the girls or John will stay.
    A: Won't he?   24
       Won't they?   21
       no reply   1

65. w: Neither John nor Tom stayed.
    A: Did he?   32
       Did they?   13
       Didn't they?   1

66. w: Neither John nor Sue stayed.
    A: Did they?   24
       Did she?   18
       Did he?   2

        Didn't they?   1
        no reply   1

67. w: Either all the boys or none of them will stay.
    a: Will they?   27
       Won't they?   17
       Will he?   2

68. w: Either none of the boys or all of them will stay.
    a: Won't they?   42
       Will they?   4

There is a normative rule for standard English that the verb agrees in number with that part of the *either* . . . *or* subject which is nearest to it; all of Walrus's statements in this section sidestep this matter since they contain verb forms that are uninflected for number. The problem faced by Alligator is whether to extend this rule to cover the gender and number of the pronoun that refers to an *either* . . . *or* subject. We observe that generally fewer than half did so. Example 59 presented no problem; since both parts of the subject are plural, the pronoun must be plural. In 60, however, although both parts of the subject are masculine singular, not everyone chose to use a masculine singular pronoun—six persons used the plural *they*, following the very convenient rule to always use a plural pronoun when referring to an *either* . . . *or* expression.

If we examine 61 and 62, we observe that about half decided to use *they* when the two parts of the subject differ in gender (slightly more when the female part is next to the verb), while the other half used the singular pronoun corresponding in gender to the part nearer the verb. Three persons, however, used the masculine singular in 61 and one person the feminine singular in 62, using the singular pronoun agreeing in gender with the part farther from the verb. One person hit upon the clever solution of repeating the disjunction in the pronominal response, while yet another copped out. Unfortunately, the exercise did not provide such a sentence as:

69. w: Either Sue or Mary will stay.

It would have been useful to have had the results of 69 to compare with those of 60.

Examples 63 and 64 contain a disjunction of singular and plural subjects. In 63, a unanimous *they* response was obtained to a disjunction in which the plural part was next to the verb; in 64, with a masculine singular part next to the verb, a slight majority used *he*, the remainder used *they*, with one person again abstaining. Examples 65 and 66 are the only ones dealing with *neither . . . nor* subjects. With both subjects masculine singular, this time only slightly more than two-thirds of the respondents used *he*; compare this result with that of 60. Similarly in 66, in which there is a disjunction of a male and a female, more respondents chose *they* than in the parallel *either . . . or* example 61. An explanation for this is proposed in Chapter 6.

Finally, examples 67 and 68 test how the respondents determine the negativity of a sentence in which half of the subject is negative. From 68 we learn that if the positive part of the subject is closer to the verb, the sentence is nearly universally judged positive; only four persons held otherwise. If the negative part is closer to the verb, less than a two-thirds majority considered the sentence as a whole negative. Two persons, moreover, treated *none of them* as deserving a masculine singular pronoun.

The last group of examples deals with the problem of determining the person, number, and gender of subjects quantified by *all*, *none*, and *each*.

70. w: All of us will stay.
   A: Won't we?   44
      Won't they?   2

71. w: None of us will stay.
   A: Will we?   42
      Will he?   2
      Shall we?   1
      Won't we?   1

72. w: Each of you will stay.
    a: Won't you?   44
       Won't he?   2
73. w: Each of the fellows will stay.
    a: Won't he?   30
       Won't they? 16
74. w: Each of us is staying.
    a: Aren't we?   34
       Isn't he?   11
       Won't we?   1

As 70 illustrates, subjects quantified by *all* pose no problems; the pronoun used to refer to them agrees with the person and gender (it must be plural) of the expression quantified. I am at a loss to explain the response "Won't they?" that two persons gave, which strikes me as a completely counter-intuitive tag question to 70; if anything, "Won't you?" would have sounded better. When the subject was quantified by *none*, again nearly everyone used the pronoun agreeing with the expression quantified. One person fussily corrected my use of *will* to *shall* for first person subjects, and another treated the sentence as positive (compare examples 30 and 31). Two replied with "Will he?" which certainly is not nearly so bad as the "Won't they?" of 70.

When the subject was quantified by *each*, there was a somewhat greater tendency to use the third person singular pronoun in response. Two-thirds used the third person singular when the expression quantified was third person plural (73), but only about one-quarter did so when it was first person plural (74) even when the verb in Walrus's statement was third person singular. Only two respondents used the third person pronoun when the expression quantified was second person plural (the verb in 72 does not happen to show agreement—I do not know how much influence this had on the respondents); everyone else used the second person.

I think that by now the reader will agree that the Walrus and Alligator game can be used quite constructively—to reveal some of the fascinating range and depth of the rules of grammar that everyone follows when he speaks and writes English, and to reveal the many differences in detail that seem to exist among individual speakers. Some of these differences, I have argued, can be attributed to disparities between the normative grammar learned and taught in the schools and the grammars that everyone has internalized from his extra-curricular activities (particularly in the preschool years). That this same conflict rages in the heads of junior high and high school teachers should be clear from the results of my class exercise. I encourage others to try the game; they will be convinced that the same holds true for themselves.

PROBLEMS AND SUGGESTIONS FOR FURTHER STUDY

1. Why would the Walrus and Alligator game not be of particular interest if played in French or German?

2. George Miller, in the reference cited at the end of Chapter 1, suggests that a game like "The Walrus and the Alligator" can be played by six-year-olds just as well as by adults (at least, they should be able to play Alligator). Try it out on any six-year-olds you can persuade to cooperate.

3. If you have access to a computer whose time you can waste, you might try to program it to play Alligator. Naturally, you will have to restrict drastically the class of sentences you use as input. I, for one, would be interested in learning what success you obtain.

4. If you decide to play the game with your friends or students, be sure to include sentences like those in exercises 17–21, using the helping verbs *can, could, shall,*

should, *might*, *dare*, and *need*. The results should be interesting.

5. Account for the origins and widespread use of the locution "Aren't I?" This topic has received some discussion in the literature.

6. Compare your response and those of the people with whom you play the game to Walrus's statement in 16, and to the following statement:

    75. w: Six books happen to be on the table.

7. As Walrus, try using examples like 42–46 with expressions such as *I suppose, I imagine, I would guess*, in place of *I think*. What sorts of results do you get?

8. Jeffrey Gruber, in his monograph "Functions of the Lexicon in Formal Descriptive Grammars," has observed that if a person or animal is referred to by name, it is generally not referred to by the neuter pronoun. Test this observation, using examples like:

    76. w: My parrakeet is sick.
    77. w: Tweety, my parrakeet, is sick.

9. What responses do you get to:

    78. w: Two plus two is four.
    79. w: Two plus two are four.

Make sure to separate these examples when you play, so that Alligator's response to one is not unduly influenced by his response to the other.

10. Like the names of ships, the names of countries evoke the feminine pronoun. Test the strength of this, using examples like:

    80. w: America will always defend her overseas interests.
    81. w: America supports the United Nations.

The fact that some countries have masculine symbols can

create a "conflict." I am told that a recent President once made an affirmation like "I assure you that Uncle Sam will always stand behind her commitments."

11. Can you think of any other cases of conflict between normative English grammar and grammar acquired outside of school which would be illustrated by "The Walrus and the Alligator"?

12. What do you think is measured by multiple-choice examinations concerning knowledge of normative English grammar, particularly those that have been used by college entrance examination boards? To what extent do you think that good performance on these exams correlates with collegiate success? With the student's overall "command" of the English language in reading, writing, public speaking, debating, and conversation? With the degree to which he complies with authority?

3

THE PROPOSITIONAL CORE OF ENGLISH

1. Sentences of the Propositional Core

In Chapter 2, it was informally shown how intricate the rules of English grammar are in the formation of tag questions and how they can vary from one group of persons to another. We now embark on a somewhat more systematic attempt to explore the nature of some grammatical rules having to do with English sentence structure in general.

There is a relatively long-standing tradition that certain types of English sentences are more elementary than others, that their fundamental character is that they are simpler in overall structure. Without yet attempting to make any of these notions precise, let me list a few examples of sentences that most grammarians would agree belong to the set of elementary English sentences:

1. The bananas are ripe.
2. My bicycle disappeared.
3. George Washington lived in this house.

4. Mother drinks dark beer.
5. Roller coasters frighten my little brother.
6. The stone dropped to the bottom.
7. The hippies were giving flowers out to the passers-by.
8. Princess Grace is the wife of Prince Rainier.
9. Harriet is aware that the boss is fond of her.
10. Snoopy realizes that he is doomed.

Most traditional grammarians would also assign particular labels to the sentences on this list. They would probably agree to call them declarative sentences and not, say, interrogative or imperative sentences; they would also label them active sentences and not passive sentences; and they would say that they are positive, or affirmative, sentences, and not negative sentences. Sentences 1 through 8 would also be called simple sentences; 9 and 10 would be called complex sentences, because each of the latter contains within it a simple sentence (one might therefore exclude 9 and 10 from the list of elementary English sentences, but I have chosen to include them for reasons given below). Moreover, none of these sentences contains within it any particularly complicated nominal expression—the expression *my little brother* in sentence 5 is probably the most involved. We would exclude from the list of elementary sentences any sentence containing a complex nominal expression such as *the dog which my sister is afraid of*, although we would be quite happy to include any sentence containing the noun *Fluffy* should that sentence happen to meet the other criteria, even though Fluffy happens to be the dog which my sister is afraid of.

Let us extrapolate from sentences 1–10 that any English sentence is elementary if it is a declarative, active, affirmative sentence not containing any complex nominal expressions, or, if it is complex, if each of the sentences contained within it is declarative, active, and affirmative. A grammarian who is also a philosopher might observe that elementary English sentences express propositions, although he would be quick to point out that a particular sentence is not to be equated with a proposition—it turns out that many different sentences can express the same proposition. For this reason, we say that any elementary English sentence belongs to the "propositional core" of English (another term for this that you may find in the linguistics literature is "kernel," but I have chosen not to adopt it, although not for any really good reason).

2. Subcategories of Propositional Core Sentences

Sentences 1–10 can also be grammatically subcategorized, mainly according to the predicates (verb, adjective, or predicate noun) occurring in them. The predicate of sentence 1 consists of the adjective *ripe*, so we may call 1 an adjectival sentence. Sentence 2 contains a simple intransitive verb as predicate, so 2 is called an intransitive sentence. Sentences 3 and 6 may be categorized in a variety of ways, depending upon how one construes the relationship between the verbs *lived* and *dropped* to the expressions that follow them: *in this house* and *to the bottom*. If one chooses to call the latter expressions adverbial, then 3 and 6 are both intransitive; if on the other hand these are viewed as locational or directional objects of the verbs, then we may be inclined to call the sentences transitive oblique (the term "oblique" refers to any object expression introduced by a preposition such as *in* or *to*, as opposed to the term "direct," referring to objects not introduced by a preposition). Sentences 4 and 5 are called transitive, since their verbs are followed by direct objects. Sentence 7 contains a verbal expression *were giving . . . out*, which is followed by two object expressions: one direct, *flowers*, and the other oblique, *to the passers-by*. The latter object is also called an indirect object, a term reserved for object expressions introduced by *to* accompanying direct objects. Sentence 7 may be called doubly transitive. Sentence 8 is an example of a predicate nominal sentence, since the predicate is the nominal expression *the wife*. It is also transitive oblique, since the predicate is followed by the nominal expression *Prince Rainier* introduced by the preposition *of* which functions as the oblique object of *wife*. Sentence 9 is an adjectival sentence, like 1, but the expression *that the boss is fond of her*, which we call a subordinate clause, functions as the direct object of the adjective. Therefore, we may call 9 both adjectival and transitive, or if you will, transitive adjectival. The subordinate clause, being itself an elementary sentence (when one takes away the *that*), can be categorized as a transitive oblique adjectival sentence. Finally, 10 is another example of a transitive sentence; it contains a subordinate clause which is an adjectival sentence.

This is a fairly complete syntactic categorization of elementary sentences in English; we might be able to add one or two more categories to the list, but there is no need for our doing that here. I say syntactic, because only characteristics of the surface structures of those sentences were taken into consideration in the classification. No attention was paid to the deep structures of any of those sentences, so that the classification can hardly be said to be semantic.

3. Relationships to Sentences outside the Core

Again, according to grammatical tradition, one can relate sentences of the propositional core to sentences outside the core by performing certain grammatical operations on them. These operations can take the form of (a) making additions or insertions of material into the core sentences, (b) making rearrangements of the constituents in core sentences, or (c) deleting constituents from core sentences. Thus, for example, we can convert the core sentences 1–10 into negative sentences by the addition or insertion of the word *not* or suffix *n't* in the appropriate places. In sentences 1, 7, 8, and 9, the negative word or suffix must be inserted after the form of the verb *be* that occurs in them, so that we obtain:

11. The bananas aren't ripe.
12. The hippies weren't giving flowers out to the passers-by.

13. Princess Grace isn't the wife of Prince Rainier.
14. Harriet isn't aware that the boss is fond of her.

In the remaining core sentences, we find that the negative word or suffix must precede the verb that occurs in them; moreover, the form of the verb *do* that is the same in tense and number as the verb in the core sentence must be inserted before the negative element, and the verb loses its inflection. We obtain:

15. My bicycle didn't disappear.
16. George Washington didn't live in this house.
17. Mother doesn't drink dark beer.
18. Roller coasters don't frighten my little brother.
19. The stone didn't drop to the bottom.
20. Snoopy doesn't realize that he is doomed.

The subordinate clauses of sentences 9 and 10 can be made negative, too, so that we also have the noncore sentences:

21. Harriet is aware that the boss isn't fond of her.
22. Snoopy realizes that he isn't doomed.
23. Harriet isn't aware that the boss isn't fond of her.
24. Snoopy doesn't realize that he isn't doomed.

A core sentence also can be converted into a simple interrogative sentence by relatively straightforward grammatical operations (a simple interrogative sentence is an interrogative sentence that is not introduced by one of the interrogative words, such as *who, what, when, why,* and so forth; another term for such a sentence is yes-no question, since such questions generally call for either a "yes" or "no" response). Sentences 1, 7, 8, and 9 are converted into simple interrogative sentences by putting at the beginning of the sentence the form of the verb *be* that occurs in them. Examples 25 and 26 below illustrate the effects of this operation on 1 and 7:

25. Are the bananas ripe?
26. Were the hippies giving flowers out to the passers-by?

This statement suffices for the written form of these questions. When spoken, 25 and 26 are also heard with a rise in the pitch of the voice toward the end, unlike the corresponding declarative sentences 1 and 7; we assume that this rise in pitch is triggered by a grammatical operation just as the word-order change is. The remaining core sentences are turned into simple interrogative sentences by the addition of the form of the verb *do* that is the same in tense and number as the verb in the core sentence, with that verb losing its inflection. Examples 27–29 below illustrate the effect of these operations on sentences 2, 4, and 5:

27. Did my bicycle disappear?
28. Does Mother drink dark beer?
29. Do roller coasters frighten my little brother?

Unlike the operations that create negative sentences, the operations that create simple interrogative sentences cannot be applied to subordinate clauses, for we do not find in the English language any sentences like:

30. *Harriet is aware that is the boss fond of her?
31. *Snoopy realizes that is he doomed?

We say that 30 and 31 are ungrammatical in English, or more simply and to the point, that they are out.

The operations that create negative and interrogative sentences can both be applied to core sentences, the results being negative interrogative sentences. Here are a few examples:

32. Aren't the bananas ripe?
33. Doesn't Mother drink dark beer?
34. Isn't Harriet aware that the boss is fond of her?

If, however, we choose to express the negative by the negative word *not*, rather than the suffix *n't*, we generally say:

35. Are the bananas not ripe?
36. Does Mother not drink dark beer?

37. Is Harriet not aware that the boss is fond of her?

We can most easily account for the form of negative interrogative sentences if we assume that the operations that separately create negative and simple interrogative sentences are both applied, and in that order, to core sentences. We must also assume that the operation for forming interrogative sentences moves to the front of the sentence the form of *do* introduced by the negative operation, together with whatever suffixes (in particular, *n't*) are attached to it, exactly as it moves the forms of the verb *be* and its suffixes. Thus, example 33 is obtained from the core sentence 4 by first making it negative (sentence 17) and then interrogative. The reader should investigate the consequences of trying to obtain negative interrogative sentences by applying the operations in the reverse order, to see what difficulties arise.

Passive sentences can only be formed from certain core sentences, transitive (and then only certain ones) or transitive oblique (again only certain ones). The operation which forms such sentences is also quite complicated—one can see this at a glance by comparing the core sentence 4 with its passive counterpart (we repeat 4 for convenience):

4. Mother drinks dark beer.
38. Dark beer is drunk by mother.

The object of the core sentence becomes the subject of the passive sentence; the form of *be* that is the same in person, number, and tense as the verb of the core sentence is inserted, and the verb is converted to its past participle; the subject of the core sentence becomes an oblique object of the past participle, introduced by the preposition *by*. Of the ten sentences, in addition to sentence 4, only 3, 5, 7, and possibly 10 have passive counterparts:

39. This house was lived in by George Washington.
40. My little brother is frightened by roller coasters.
41. Flowers were being given out to passers-by by the hippies.

42. ?That he is doomed is realized by Snoopy.[1]

Notice that 6 does not have a clearly grammatical passive counterpart; what one obtains by applying the passive-sentence operation to it is:

43. *The bottom was dropped to by the stone.

In my judgment, 43 merits the asterisk, although some readers may feel I am being too harsh. The same is true for the passive counterpart to this sentence (a variation of 3):

44. George Washington lived in Virginia.

which is:

45. *Virginia was lived in by George Washington.

My impression is that it is all right to use a passive sentence to say that houses are lived in, but not states of the Union. We shall have more to say on this topic in Chapter 6, Section 8; my purpose here has been served by merely noting the examples.

Finally, to illustrate the operation of deletion, let us consider how imperative sentences are formed from core sentences. Imperative sentences are not formed from sentences like 1–10, but rather from sentences containing the subject *you*. Thus, the imperative:

46. Take these clothes to the laundry.

is formed from the core sentence:

47. You take these clothes to the laundry.

and not, say, from:

48. People take these clothes to the laundry.

The operation involved is, clearly, the deletion of the sub-

---

[1] A question mark preceding a sentence indicates that, in the author's judgment at least, the sentence is of dubious grammatical status, not clearly out, but not clearly in either.

ject. What is the syntactic motivation for viewing the formation of imperatives in this way? Consider an imperative sentence like:

49. Wash yourself behind the ears.

Notice that the direct object of the verb is the second-person reflexive pronoun. In core sentences, the only occasion in which a reflexive pronoun appears as a direct object is when the subject is of the same person, number and gender. For example:

50. I wash myself behind the ears.
51. Harry washes himself behind the ears.
52. The Russians wash themselves behind the ears.

We never find sentences like:

53. *I wash himself behind the ears.
54. *The Russians wash ourselves behind the ears.

Therefore, we explain the fact that in imperative sentences the only reflexive direct objects are in the second person (and conversely that no other person is ever expressed by a reflexive object) by assuming that all imperative sentences are obtained from core sentences in which the subject is in the second person.

4. Early Generative-Transformational Theory

The traditional view that I have been expounding—that there exists a set of elementary sentences in English of a particularly simple syntactic form, and a set of syntactic operations that convert those sentences into all the other possible sentences having generally a more complicated form —was developed during the 1950s into an explicit theory of language, primarily by Zellig Harris of the University of Pennsylvania and his student Noam Chomsky, now of the Massachusetts Institute of Technology. Differences quickly developed between Harris's and Chomsky's theoretical view-points, but rather than attempt to deal with them here, I will simply present the position formulated by Chomsky in his well-known monograph *Syntactic Structures*, which has had far greater influence among linguists and educators. Chomsky assumes that there is a set of syntactic rules that can be thought of as creating, or generating, structures that directly underlie the sentences of the propositional core. These rules, he argues, must furthermore be of a particular form, such as to provide an analysis of a sentence into its constituent parts. He calls this body of rules the constituent (or phrase) structure component of the grammar. The structures that they generate can be represented by any of the notational techniques familiar to grammarians, such as traditional diagramming, but Chomsky chose to develop a notation much more suitable for his theoretical purposes, namely, the tree (or branching) diagram. A tree diagram that one might wish to associate with core sentence 6 is shown in Figure 2.

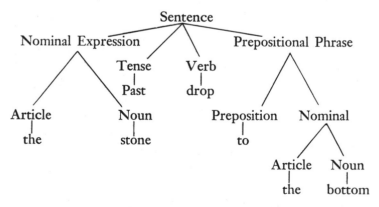

Figure 2.   Tree diagram of sentence 6.

Before continuing, let me point out that the structure of Figure 2 is not to be taken as the surface structure of sentence 6 but as a representation of a structure which underlies the sentence to be parsed. The reason that Figure 2 looks very much like a suitable parsing of 6 is that few rules of the next component are applicable to it.

The structures emanating from the constituent structure component of the grammar then pass through the next component of the grammar, the transformational component, which consists of rules, called transformations, that operate on those structures. The transformational component of English, according to Chomsky, includes, among others, the operations we have been considering above to create negative, interrogative, passive, and imperative sentences. These rules are assumed to be ordered with respect to one another, so that a sentence that is the result of the application of several rules has undergone the operations in a fixed order. Finally, it is assumed that all transformations are limited by constraints on what they can do. Thus, while it is permitted for a transformation to move a particular constituent of a sentence to the beginning of the sentence (as is done by the interrogative transformation), one could not have a transformation that would, say, interchange the position of every other word in a sentence; and while a transformation may delete a particular constituent in a sentence (as the imperative transformation does), no transformation is allowed, say, to delete every other word of a sentence. In Chomsky's view, these constraints are part of universal grammar; they limit and guide the child in his attempt to determine the grammar of the language he is in the process of acquiring.

The transformational rules we informally considered above are actually illustrative of just one sort of transformational rule. They are what may be called optional, meaning-changing transformations. They are called optional because if they are not applied, the structures to which they are not applied still come out as sentences of English. In other words, one may apply a transformation such as the negative transformation to a structure, but one does not have to. They are called meaning-changing because, obviously (except in the case of the passive transformation, where it is not so obvious), the sentence that results from the application of one of these transformations can, and generally does, mean something quite different from the sentence that results from the nonapplication of that transformation. No one, I am sure, would say that sentences 1 and 11 mean the same thing!

Transformations of another type are both obligatory and meaning-preserving. For example, in *Syntactic Structures* Chomsky describes a transformation which attaches the tense constituent, such as the one in Figure 2, as a suffix to the following verbal constituent; in this case Past $+$ *drop* is transformed into *drop* $+$ Past, which is ultimately realized as *dropped*. This transformation is obligatory, because given the way Chomsky sets up the constituent structure rules for English sentences, tense constituents always precede the verbs with which they are associated (he does this for very sound reasons, which, however, I will not discuss here), whereas in the realizations of these sentences, they always follow or are absorbed into those verbs. The rule is meaning-preserving because the operation it effects has no bearing on the meaning of the sentence itself. It is a purely syntactic phenomenon.

A third set of transformations are optional and meaning-preserving; such rules may also be called stylistic transformations, and the two sentences which result, one from the application of one of these transformations and the other from its nonapplication, may be called stylistic variants. If one compares sentence 7, which I repeat below, with 55, one recognizes that they differ only in their surface syntactic form, not in meaning:

7. The hippies were giving flowers out to the passers-by.
55. The hippies were giving out flowers to the passers-by.

Suppose we decide that the structure associated with 55 should be taken as that assigned by the constituent-structure component of the grammar (this is not quite right, since past tense has already been attached to *be*, and *ing* suffixed to *give* by obligatory transformations, but let us overlook this

for purposes of discussion). Then 7 can be obtained by the application of a stylistic transformation which moves the word *out* from its position next to the verb to a position following the direct object *flowers.*
Next, consider sentences 56 and 57:

56. The hippies were selling the passers-by flowers.
57. The hippies were selling flowers to the passers-by.

The form of 56 can be accounted for by postulating the operation of another stylistic transformation which moves the indirect object to a position immediately following the verb, and which deletes the preposition *to.*

The fourth sort of transformation that Chomsky postulates in *Syntactic Structures* takes two sentences and puts them together into one, either as a compound sentence such as:

58. The dish ran away with the spoon and the cow jumped over the moon.

from the separate sentences:

59. The dish ran away with the spoon.
60. The cow jumped over the moon.

or as a complex sentence such as:

61. The dog which my sister is afraid of weighs ten pounds.

from the sentences:

62. The dog weighs ten pounds.
63. My sister is afraid of the dog.

Chomsky calls this type generalized transformations. Sentences such as 9 and 10 could also be viewed as resulting from a generalized transformation, for example, one which substitutes the subordinate clause for a pronoun functioning as a direct or oblique object. We could obtain 9 from the two sentences:

64. Harriet is aware of it.

65. The boss is fond of her.

(Note that the preposition *of* is deleted in the process of forming 9.) Sentence 10 would be the result of substituting 67 for the pronoun direct object of 66:

66. Snoopy realizes it.
67. He is doomed.

In fact, just such a view is espoused by Chomsky in *Syntactic Structures* and in an article written a year later entitled "A Transformational Approach to Syntax," which appears in Jerry A. Fodor and Jerrold J. Katz (eds.), *The Structure of Language*. We have not followed Chomsky on this point, however, because there are a number of sentences like 9 and 10 for which there is no grammatical sentence containing a pronoun for which the clause can be substituted. For example:

68. It seems that the boss is fond of Harriet.
69. *It seems it.
70. The boss is fond of Harriet.

We call the theory outlined in *Syntactic Structures* the early generative-transformational theory: "early" to distinguish it from approaches developed later (to be discussed in Chapter 4), and "generative-transformational" because it views the rules of grammar as creating, or generating, the structures of sentences of a language and because the transformational component is an important and distinguishing hallmark of the theory. The theory also considers that there is a phonological component of the sort described in Chapter 1, but it does not make the distinction between semantics and syntax that we drew in Chapter 2 and outlined in Figure 1, page 7. According to the theory, all the rules of grammar are syntactic but some have semantic consequences (the constituent-structure rules and the meaning-changing transformations). The relationships among the various components are diagrammed in Figure 3.

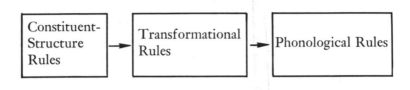

Figure 3. Interrelations among the components of a grammar according to early generative-transformational theory (compare Fig. 1, p. 7).

The most comprehensive treatment of English grammar from the early generative-transformational viewpoint is to be found in Robert B. Lees, *The Grammar of English Nominalizations*, and it is this viewpoint which has been represented to the world of education by the many works of Paul Roberts. It is also to some extent the viewpoint described in Emmon Bach, *An Introduction to Transformational Grammars*; Andreas Koutsoudas, *Writing Transformational Grammars*; and Owen Thomas, *Transformational Grammar and the Teacher of English*. In subsequent chapters, we shall not be following this particular linguistic theory, nor shall we even be following in detail what may be called later generative-transformational theory; but before discussing the theoretical approach we shall be following and the reasons for our not adopting other approaches, let us examine more closely some of the properties of the sentences we have already agreed belong to the propositional core of English.

5. Predicates and Variables

The heart of a sentence belonging to the propositional core is its predicate—the main verb, adjective, or (predicate) noun occurring in it. We can appreciate this most easily by considering that we can substitute meaningless tokens, for example, numerals or letters of the alphabet, for the subject and objects of any core sentence, and still make sense:

71. x disappeared.
72. x lived in y.
73. x were giving y out to z.
74. x are ripe.
75. x is the wife of y.
76. x is aware that y is fond of x.
77. x realizes that x is doomed.

If, however, we retain the lexical content of the subject and objects, but replace the predicate with a letter of the alphabet, the result communicates next to nothing:

78. My bicycle x.
79. George Washington x in that house.
80. The hippies were x-ing flowers out to the passers-by.
81. The bananas are x.
82. Princess Grace is the x of Prince Rainier.
83. Harriet is x that the boss is y of her.
84. Snoopy x that he is y.

Of these, only 80 and 82 come close to conveying anything, but they do so because one can make a reasonable guess at what the predicate must be; only a verb such as *give* or *pass* can substitute for x in 80, and a kinship noun such as *wife* or *cousin* is about the only reasonable substitute for x in 82. But in 71 through 77, one need not make guesses about what the x's, y's, and z's stand for in order to make sense of the sentences.

Examples 71–77 look very much like propositions in symbolic logic, in which the verbs, adjectives, and nouns are functioning as predicates and the x's, y's, and z's are functioning as variables, the entities which stand in some relationship to the predicates. To make the expressions look more like what a logician is used to, we can "translate" them into representations such as:

85. Disappeared (x).
86. Lived (x, y).
87. Was giving out (x, y, z).
88. Ripe (x).
89. Wife (x, y).
90. Aware $[x, \text{Fond } (y, x)]$.
91. Realizes $[x, \text{Doomed } (x)]$.

The translation consists of shifting the predicates to the beginning of the sentence, and putting the variables associated with them into following parentheses. The variables are left in the same order as they appear in the core sentence, but the prepositions, articles (such as *the* in 75), and the forms of the verb *be* have been omitted. The subordinate clauses of 76 and 77, it will have been noted, have been treated as ordinary objects of their respective predicates, and have themselves been cast into the same form, with their own predicates put first. When saying something like 85 aloud, one says "Disappeared of *x*"; something more complicated, such as 90, would come out sounding like "Aware of *x*, fond of *y*, *x*."

This translation is useful for illustrating that different predicates in English differ in the number of variables that can occur together with them. Thus, *disappeared* and *ripe* occur with only one variable; *lived*, *wife*, *aware*, and *realizes* occur with two; *was giving out*, with three. The grammatical label "intransitive" is appropriate for predicates that occur with one variable, "transitive" for those with two, and "doubly transitive" for those with three. Since the translation suppresses prepositions and ignores parts of speech, the grammatical notions direct, indirect, and oblique, and the notions adjectival and nominal, are not revealed in the translation. The translation suggests that we can replace the grammatical labels by others perhaps more revealing; we may call predicates with one variable one-place predicates, those with two, two-place predicates, and so on. This would make logicians happy, since they use the terms "transitive" and "intransitive" in ways that differ from those of traditional grammarians—

by scrapping the grammatical labels, we avoid potential terminological confusions. Also, the new terminology automatically provides a label for a predicate no matter how many variables are associated with it, whereas the grammatical terminology cuts out above three variables. A typical four-place predicate in English is the verb *buy*, as in the sentence:

92. John buys washing machines from the factory for $150.

which becomes, upon substitution of variables:

93. *x* buys *y* from *z* for *w*.

which is translated:

94. Buys (*x*, *y*, *z*, *w*).

It should be emphasized that the exercise of translating English sentences into this logical notation serves no useful linguistic function other than to clarify the notion of the number of variables a predicate can have, and to illustrate some properties regarding the formation of complex sentences (which we are shortly coming to). Because prepositions are suppressed, two very different propositions can be translated into the same logical expression; for example, both 95 and 96 below come out as 97:

95. *x* rents *y* to *z*.
96. *x* rents *y* from *z*.
97. Rents (*x*, *y*, *z*).

But clearly it is *z* who gets *y* in 95, and *x* who gets *y* in 96.

Expressions 90 and 91 illustrate one important way in which complex expressions may be built up out of simple ones, and, given our limitations on the propositional core, the only way that complex expressions can arise within that core. Despite this limitation, notice that it is possible to build up arbitrarily complex expressions by repeatedly inserting a proposition as an object of a predicate such as *realizes* or *aware*. Thus, besides 90 and 91, we can obtain:

98. Realizes$\Big(x, \text{Aware} \Big\{ y, \text{Believes } [z, \text{Fond } (v, w)] \Big\} \Big)$.

which, translating back into English and putting in nominal expressions for the variables, comes out looking like:

99. Harriet realizes that the preacher is aware that my sister believes that Snoopy is fond of artichoke hearts.

From this it follows that the number of sentences in the propositional core of English is infinite.

Subordinate clauses can also function in English as subjects of predicates. For example, consider the sentences:

100. That the bananas are ripe is obvious.
101. That Snoopy realizes that he is doomed amazes Charlie Brown.

which upon substitution of variables for the nominal expressions are translated as:

102. Obvious [Ripe (x)].
103. Amazes $\Big\{ \text{Realizes } [x, \text{Doomed } (x)], y \Big\}$.

By repeatedly inserting propositions as subjects of such predicates as *amazes*, *obvious*, *upsets*, and so forth, we find that we can create sentences that completely follow the rules of English syntax but that are completely unintelligible if read, and more dramatically unintelligible if spoken. By doing it twice we obtain ponderous, but not unintelligible sentences, for example:

104. That that mother drinks dark beer upsets father is obvious.

But by doing it three times, we obtain such mind-bogglers as:

105. That that that mother drinks dark beer upsets father amazes the preacher is not true.

And one can imagine the results of doing it more than three times (such examples can only be constructed—and figured out—by using pencil and paper).

This completes our syntactic account of the sentences of the propositional core of English, and of their relationships to other, less elementary and generally more complicated sentences of the language. To obtain further insights into their nature, we find that we must abandon the purely syntactic framework of early generative-transformational grammar, and look at these sentences and their relationships to others from a point of view that assigns priority to semantics. This we set out to do in the next chapter.

PROBLEMS AND
SUGGESTIONS FOR
FURTHER STUDY²

1. The discussion in Section 2 of this chapter departs from traditional grammar by calling the nominal expressions that follow adjectives and predicate nouns objects of those adjectives and nouns. Why is this departure justified?

2. Give arguments to support the contention that the genitive expression *Prince Rainier's* in sentence 106 below is the object of the noun it modifies:

   106. Princess Grace is Prince Rainier's wife.

3. Why must the negative transformation be formulated so as to insert the negative element after the first helping verb in a sentence?

4. Explain how Chomsky in *Syntactic Structures* accounts for the insertion of *do* in negative and interrogative sentences.

---

² A dagger before a problem indicates that it is somewhat more difficult than the others, and may be passed over if the reader wishes.

5. Relate the discussion in Chapter 2 of the status of *have* as a helping verb to the problem of generating negative and interrogative sentences that contain this verb.

6. How is the passive transformation ordered with respect to the interrogative and negative transformations?

7. Give an example of transitive verbs (those which occur with direct objects in core sentences) that cannot occur in passive sentences.

8. Show that there are transitive verbs that have the same property as *live* with respect to the passive transformation (consider examples 3, 39, 44, and 45). Hint—start by considering synonyms of *live* whose objects are not oblique.

9. Can you find syntactic arguments other than the one that was given in the text for contending that the imperative transformation deletes a second-person subject? Does that subject necessarily have to be the form *you*? (On the latter question, see J. L. Thorne, "English Imperative Sentences.")

10. What is the order of the negative transformation with respect to the imperative transformation? Can you think of any way of accounting for the *do* in the prohibition:

    107. Don't be a fool.

    For a very thorough, but somewhat difficult, discussion of the imperative construction in English, see Dwight L. Bolinger, "Imperatives in English."

11. Suppose, in the game of "The Walrus and the Alligator" (Chapter 2), we also allow Walrus to use imperative sentences. How would you, as Alligator, reply to:

    108. w: Give me some help.
    109. w: Don't tell Fred what I'm going to do.

    Give an argument which, on the basis of these examples,

supports the contention that second-person subjects are deleted transformationally in imperative sentences. Do the examples also support an argument that a particular helping verb is also deleted in the derivation of imperative sentences?

Are there imperative sentences for which there is no natural Alligator reply? Give some examples, and see if you can determine what properties distinguish such sentences from those that do, like 108 and 109, have natural Alligator replies.

12. How would you, as Alligator, reply to hortatory sentences, such as:

   110. w: Let's go to the movies this afternoon.
   111. w: Let's not [don't let's] take your kid sister along.

   Give an analysis of hortatory sentences along the lines of *Syntactic Structures*.

13. Harris's conception of a grammar has been most thoroughly set forth in his articles "Cooccurrence and Transformation in Linguistic Analysis" and "Transformational Theory."

14. For an introductory, but formal, discussion of the notions-constituent-structure rule and the transformational rule, see Bach, *An Introduction to Transformational Grammars*, Peters, "What Is Mathematical Linguistics?" and my article "Formal Linguistic Theory and the Theory of Automata," in Bever and Weksel (eds.), *The Structure and Psychology of Language*. The latter also contains a discussion of the problem of the unintelligibility of certain grammatical sentences, as does Chomsky, *Aspects of the Theory of Syntax*, Chapter 1, and George Miller and S. Isard, "Free Recall of Self-embedded English Sentences."

15. Let us call the stylistic transformaiton which moves the particle *out* in sentence 7 the particle-movement transformation. Give examples that show that this rule is

obligatory when the direct object is a pronoun. Under these conditions we would have to agree that particle movement is obligatory and meaning-preserving.

16. In addition to examples 7 and 55, consider the following:

> 112. *The hippies were giving the passers-by out flowers.
> 113. *The hippies were giving the passers-by flowers out.
> 114. *The hippies were giving flowers to the passers-by out.
> 115. ?The hippies were giving out the passers-by flowers.

Show that the ungrammaticality of examples 112–115 is best accounted for by making the rule that moves the indirect object next to the verb inapplicable in case the verb is accompanied by a particle.

17. Are there conditions under which the indirect-object-movement transformation cannot be applied? Consider doubly transitive sentences in which the direct object is a pronoun. On the other hand, are there conditions under which it is obligatory? Consider sentences in which the direct object is a subordinate clause, for example:

> 116. I told the man that I was going to the store.

18. The indirect-object-movement transformation does not apply to certain doubly transitive sentences, for example:

> 117. I said some words to the judge.

Show that whether or not the rule is applicable depends on the main verb.

19. There is, apparently, an optional meaning-preserving transformation which deletes the phrase *by someone* or *by something* in passive sentences. Show how this rule applies in the creation of the sentences:

118. The shed was broken into.
119. The child was crippled.

20. Example 119 above is ambiguous; it is either the passive of the core sentence:

    120. Someone/something crippled the child.

    or is itself a core sentence in which *crippled* is simply an adjective (which happens to be pronounced and spelled just like the past participle of the verb *cripple*). Give two unambiguous sentences, each of which has roughly the same meaning as one of the meanings of 119. We call each sentence a paraphrase of one meaning of the original 119.

21. Is sentence 121 below a passive or a core sentence, and why?

    121. The furniture was unharmed by the move.

22. The word *that*, which introduces subordinate clauses that function as direct objects, may optionally be deleted. Give examples that show this to be true. Are there, however, core sentences containing such clauses to which the rule is inapplicable? If so, why is the rule inapplicable? Hint—consider such sentences as:

    122. The teacher joked that his students were anarchists.

23. The question-word interrogative transformation is responsible for creating questions like 123 out of core sentences like 124:

    123. What did you say to the judge?
    124. You said something to the judge.

    Give a precise account of how this transformation operates, and show why a form of *do* is not introduced into sentences when the subject is interrogated:

    125. Someone lived in that house.
    126. Who lived in that house?

For help on this, consult *Syntactic Structures*.

†24. The question-word interrogative transformation is capable of drawing a question-word out of a subordinate object clause, as 127 and 128 illustrate:

127. Harriet believes that the boss loves someone.
128. Whom does Harriet believe that the boss loves?

What do examples 129–131 show concerning the order of the question-word interrogative transformation with respect to the transformation that deletes *that* discussed in problem 20?

129. Harriet thinks that someone loves her.
130. *Who does Harriet think that loves her?
131. Who does Harriet think loves her?

†25. Is the question-word interrogative transformation capable of drawing a question-word out of a subordinate subject clause?

26. Sentence 42 can be improved grammatically by the application of a stylistic transformation that moves the entire subject clause to the end of the sentence in which it occurs and puts the word *it* in its place. This operation was given the name "extraposition" by the great Danish traditional grammarian Otto Jespersen, and is the subject of an intensive study by Peter S. Rosenbaum, *The Grammar of English Predicate Complement Constructions*. The effect of the extraposition transformation on 42 is:

132. It is realized by Snoopy that he is doomed.

Extraposition is obligatory when the subordinate clause is the subject of a small class of verbs; list some of these verbs. Hint—consider example 67.

†27. Is the question-word interrogative transformation capable of drawing a question-word out of an extraposed subject clause? For some discussion of this question and question

23, see Lees, *The Grammar of English Nominalizations*, Chapter 3.

28. Do you think Walrus's statements in examples 42–44 of Chapter 2 are stylistic variants? If so, formulate a stylistic transformation that shows them to be such. What positions in a sentence can be occupied by parenthetical expressions?

29. Many of the exercises that Paul Roberts would have his students do consist of working out the details of the generation of sentences, using constituent structure and transformational rules. Do you see any point to such exercises?

30. Besides 95 and 96, there are many other pairs of English sentences that differ in meaning but which have the same translation into our logical notation. Give a few examples of such pairs.

31. Why, when dealing with the translation back into English of the expression:

    133. Gave (x, y, z)

    do we have to have a convention regarding whether that sentence should have undergone the indirect-object-movement transformation? Why must we have a similar convention regarding the translation from English to our logical notation?

†32. Examples 104 and 105 can be made much more intelligible by the application of extraposition. Give some of the stylistic variants of these examples that show the application of extraposition. Does the fact of their greater intelligibility shed light on the question why there is an extraposition transformation in English grammar in the first place? For some further discussion, see my article "The Accessibility of Deep Structures," in Roderick Jacobs and Peter S. Rosenbaum (eds.), *Reading in English Transformational Grammar*.

4
ROLES AND ROLE STRUCTURE

1. Later Generative-Transformational Theory

In 1963, Jerry Fodor and Jerrold Katz published an article entitled "The Structure of a Semantic Theory" (since reprinted in their reader *The Structure of Language*), in which they noted that a complete description of a language must include an account of the meaning of its sentences. Accordingly, they postulated the existence within grammars of a semantic component, the function of which is to provide a semantic interpretation of the structures generated by the syntactic components of the sort postulated by Chomsky in *Syntactic Structures*. The rules of semantic interpretation begin with the meanings of the individual lexical items appearing in a sentence, and they construct the meanings of sentences by amalgamating these lexical meanings in accordance with the constituent structure of the sentence. At about the same time, a number of other grammarians, notably Robert Lees and Edward Klima, were showing that various supposedly optional meaning-changing transformations must be considered to be obligatory meaning-preserving ones. For example, Lees argued in *The Grammar of English Nominalizations* that the constituent-structure component, not the transformational component, must provide the negative element that appears in negative sentences; the function of the negative transformation is merely to position that element with respect to the other constituents in the surface structure of the sentence. Other arguments in support of this were advanced by Klima in his article "Negation in English" (which also appears in the Fodor and Katz reader).

In their book *An Integrated Theory of Linguistic Descriptions*, Jerrold Katz and Paul Postal gathered together the arguments then known for eliminating optional meaning-changing transformations, and adding to these a few more of their own, argued that every single such transformation that had been proposed in the literature up to that time could be eliminated in favor of introducing constituents in the constituent-structure component and making all transformations meaning-preserving. If correct, this meant that the semantic component that had been postulated by Katz and Fodor could be viewed as merely interpreting the structures generated by the constituent-structure component, the transformational operations having no effect on the meanings of sentences. Katz and Postal also speculated about the possibility of eliminating generalized transformations in favor of generating compound and complex structures directly by constituent-structure rules (as we in part suggested in Chapter 3).

Finally, Chomsky, in *Aspects of the Theory of Syntax*, brought all these ideas together and advocated a theory of grammar in which a grammatical description is organized as in Figure 4. We call this the later generative-transformational theory. The output of the constituent-structure and lexical components (for various reasons, he now viewed the lexicon as separate from the constituent-structure component) Chomsky called deep structures; the output of the transformational

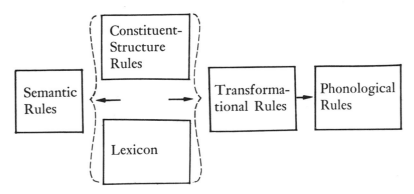

Figure 4. Interrelations among the components of a grammar according to later generative-transformational theory (compare Fig. 1, p. 7, and Fig. 3, p. 46).

component he called surface structures. Comparing Figure 4 with Figure 1 (p. 7), one will observe that they are the same, except that the semantic component in Figure 1 does the work that the semantic and constituent-structure components do together in Figure 4. It should also be pointed out that Chomsky saw various reasons for not entirely denying the semantic relevance of transformational rules (or even of phonological rules); it is possible therefore that there may be arrows connecting the transformational and phonological components with the semantic component in Figure 4, although the potential semantic relevance of these components was viewed as being quite small.

2. Roles

One serious difficulty with the linguistic theory of *Aspects* is that the semantic component is obliged to work with the traditional grammatical notions—subject, direct and indirect object, oblique object, and so forth—whereas the semantic relationship of a predicate to the nominal expressions that go with it is largely independent of these grammatical notions. The semantic relationships are most easily and directly described in terms of *roles*—as if each sentence were a miniature drama, whose plot is given by the main predicate and whose actors (in their various roles) are the nominal expressions that occur with them. The terminology for describing the role relations of variables to predicates is less fixed than the terminology for stating the syntactic relations, but we do have some tradition to guide us. The individual (or individuals) responsible for carrying out the plot is called the agent; the person or thing affected, the patient; the thing (tool, device) used by the agent, the instrument. We also have such roles as goal, source or origin, location, direction, and result. Roles can be thought of as labels for the variables that stand in relation to predicates.

It will be our contention that deep structures should be stated in terms of role relationships rather than syntactic relationships, and that nominal expressions are put into syntactic relationship by transformational rules.

First, let us examine some sentences that illustrate the possible lack of correspondence between roles and syntactic relationships.

1. John sent the news to the Congressman by telegram.
   x y z w

2. The Congressman received the news from John
   z y x
   by telegram.
   w

3. The news reached the Congressman by telegram.
   y z w

4. A telegram conveyed the news to the Congressman.
   w y z

I have underlined the nominal expressions in 1–4 that stand

in particular relations to the various predicates (which have not been underlined) and have placed an identifying letter of the alphabet under each. Each of these nominal expressions plays the same role every time it appears (except for *John*— see the discussion below), although the syntactic relations are different in the various sentences. In sentence 1, *John* plays the role of agent (x), and in 2 the related role of source. *The news* in all four sentences plays the role of patient (y), even though it occurs as a direct object in 1, 2, and 4 and as a subject in 3. *The Congressman* is goal (z) in all four sentences, despite its being an indirect object in 1, a subject in 2, a direct object in 3, and an oblique object in 4. *Telegram*, or *a telegram*, is instrument (w) in all four sentences, although it is an oblique object in 1, 2, and 3, and a subject in 4.

We conclude that the deep structure of a sentence of the propositional core in English must identify the main predicate and the roles that are associated with it. The deep structure of 1, for example, will state that the main predicate is *sent*, and that it occurs in relation to the four roles agent, patient, goal, and instrument. In a similar way, the lexical representation of the predicate *sent* (it will actually be entered in the dictionary as *send*; for the present, however, we shall ignore matters having to do with the tense of verbs) will indicate that it can occur in deep structures together with the four roles. Transformational rules will be responsible for assigning to the agent the syntactic relation of subject of *sent*, to the patient the direct-object relation, to the goal the indirect-object relation, and to the instrument the oblique-object relation (with the preposition *by*). The same sorts of observations can be made about 2–4.

Next, let us look at pairs of closely related sentences in which the same roles are used but in different syntactic relationships to the various predicates.

   5. I like your outfit.
   6. Your outfit pleases me.

Clearly, the two predicates *like* and *please* are close in meaning; furthermore, they occur with nominal expressions that play the same roles, which we can identify as patient (expressed by *I* or *me*—this time it is person, not thing, affected) and stimulus (expressed by *your outfit*). More idiomatic examples of the same sort are:

7. My roommate digs Paul Klee.
8. Paul Klee sends my roommate.

Another pair of examples of this sort, this time with the same predicate occurring in each, is:

9. The audience thrilled to the candidate's speech.
10. The candidate's speech thrilled the audience.

Now consider the pair:

11. I just realized that the muffins must be burning.
12. It just occurred to me that the muffins must be burning.

In 11, we would again identify the role of the subject *I* as patient; it is not entirely clear, however, exactly what to call the role of the object clause *that the muffins must be burning*, and unfortunately there is no clear traditional terminology to guide us at this point. Let us simply assign it the role of "observation," however unsatisfactorily that label might impress us. Nevertheless, the same roles turn up in 12; this time the patient occurs as the oblique object with the preposition *to*, and the observation as subject (which has, however, been extraposed—see problem 26 of Chapter 3).

The various roles limit the kinds of nominal expression that can be used to express them. For example, for someone or something to be an agent, it must be capable of acting on its own volition, and since inanimate physical objects or abstract ideas normally cannot do so, it is generally odd to use a nominal expression which refers to an inanimate object or abstract idea as an agent, as in the sentences:

13. The boulder sent the news to the Congressman by telegram.
14. Sincerity sent the news to the Congressman by telegram.

We can think of 13 and 14 as containing violations of semantic propriety—we know that an inanimate object such as boulder on an abstraction such as sincerity cannot send messages to Congressmen (of course, 14 would not be odd if *Sincerity* were to be taken as the name of a person, but this is another matter). Chomsky recognized the linguistic significance of limitations of this sort, and in *Aspects* gave them the name selectional restrictions, because he considered them to be restrictions on the selection of particular nominal expressions for subjects and objects of particular predicates. We regard examples 13 and 14 as ungrammatical but not unsyntactic, and for this reason we withhold the use of the prefixed asterisk or the question mark, which we have reserved for the marking of syntactically deviant examples.

Chomsky also used the concept of selectional restriction to deal with limitations of a somewhat different sort, for example, the limitation that the direct object of a verb like *drink* must express something drinkable, usually liquid. Thus, we would doubtless all agree that there is something quite odd semantically about this sentence:

15. Harry drank a boulder for breakfast.

since, normally, boulders (even molten boulders!) cannot be drunk. But this limitation cannot be viewed as a consequence of the fact that the object of *drink* plays the role of patient, since there are other sentences in English in which *a boulder* can be used as patient, such as:

16. Superman crushed a boulder in his bare hands.

There is another difference, too, between limitations of this sort and limitations on the roles nominal expressions can play. If we consider the sentence:

17. Harry drank the stuff for breakfast.

we understand that the material designated by the expression *the stuff* must be drinkable, and hence liquid, although ordinarily that expression does not have to designate a liquid. That it designates a liquid is assumed of *the stuff* by its use as patient of the predicate *drink*, and we say that the interpretation of the patient of the verb *drink* as something drinkable represents an assumption. Assumptions are always direct consequences of the details of the meanings of predicates. The violation of assumptions, and, to a lesser extent, limitations, concerning what can be used to express particular roles is the basis for many figures of speech. For example:

18. Harry drinks attention like a fish drinks water.

3. Role Structures

Just as it is instructive to consider how expressions designating the same role turn up in different syntactic relations to different predicates, it is useful to examine the roles found in different sentences having the same predicate (such examples have already been given in sentences 9 and 10). Consider the following examples, the main predicate of each being the verb *strike*:

19. The carpenter struck the nail with the hammer.
$\quad\quad\quad\quad x \quad\quad\quad\quad\quad y \quad\quad\quad\quad z$

20. The carpenter struck the nail.
$\quad\quad\quad\quad x \quad\quad\quad\quad\quad y$

21. The carpenter struck with the hammer.
$\quad\quad\quad\quad x \quad\quad\quad\quad\quad z$

22. The hammer struck the nail.
$\quad\quad\quad\quad z \quad\quad\quad\quad\quad y$

23. The hammer struck.
$\quad\quad\quad\quad z$

In these examples, *the carpenter* plays the agent role, *the hammer* is instrument, and *the nail* plays a multiple role. On the one hand, *the nail* is patient, because it is the object affected; on the other hand it is location, because it specifies where the hammer struck. We say that *the nail* has the multiple role patient/location. These can be separately expressed, as in the sentence:

24. The carpenter struck the nail on the head.

in which case *the nail* is patient, and *the head* is location, but notice that we do not have any sentence like:

25. *The carpenter struck on the head.

Example 19 shows that the predicate *strike* can be used with three accompanying roles: agent, instrument, and patient/location. Example 20 shows that the expression designating the instrument role can be omitted in the surface form of sentences whose main predicate is *strike*; but if we reflect on what that sentence means, we realize that an instrument is understood—the carpenter must have struck the nail with something, but this "something" has not been expressed. We conclude that in the deep structure of 20, three roles are mentioned, but that on the surface, only two are expressed, the instrumental expression having been deleted by a transformational rule. Similarly, example 21 has only two roles expressed in its surface form, but has the same three as 19 and 20 in its deep structure, the patient/location having been deleted.

Sentence 22 is ambiguous (see item 20 at the end of Chapter 3, where this term is introduced). One possible interpretation for the sentence assigns the instrument role to the *hammer*, and the patient/location role to the *nail*, the unspecified agent having been deleted. The other interpretation assigns to both *the hammer* and *the nail* the role of patient, there being no other roles in either the deep or the surface structure of the sentence. Sentence 23 is unambiguous: *the hammer* is instrument, both agent and patient/location having been deleted.

If we now reexamine sentence 20, we observe that it, like 22, is ambiguous, though in a slightly different way. We have already given one interpretation, according to which *the carpenter* is agent and *the nail* is patient. According to the other interpretation, *the carpenter* and *the nail* are both patients.

Now let us attempt to state as precisely as we can the roles with which the predicate *strike* can occur in the deep structures of propositional core sentences. First, it can occur together with the three roles agent, instrument, and patient/location, as in sentences 19, 21, and 23, and in one interpretation of sentences 20 and 22. Second, it can occur with two (or possibly more) elements in the role of patient, as in one interpretation of sentences 20 and 22. Let us say that the list of roles with which a particular predicate can occur is its role structure. The fact that the predicate *strike* can occur with the three roles agent, instrument, and patient/location may be represented by the formula in 26a:

26a. *strike*: Agent, Instrument, Patient/Location

The fact that it can also occur with two or more elements in the patient role may be represented by the formula in 26b:

26b. *strike*: ⟨Patient⟩

The notation ⟨Patient⟩ is intended simply to designate a set consisting of two or more patients. The two parts of 26 can then be put together into a composite formula 26c which expresses completely the role structure of the predicate *strike*:

26c. *strike*: $\left\{ \begin{array}{l} \text{Agent, Instrument, Patient/Location} \\ \langle\text{Patient}\rangle \end{array} \right\}$

Formula 26c can be thought of as representing a small part of what might be put into an ideal dictionary representation of the predicate *strike*. Such an entry would also include, of course, the part of speech of this predicate (namely, verb), and details about its meaning.

It will be observed that there is a particularly simple relationship between role structures and the deep structures of propositional core sentences. All that such deep structures contain that role structures do not are the nominal expressions that represent the various roles, and information about the tense and aspect of the predicate. Moreover, it is clear that verbs which are similar in meaning are very likely to have the same, or nearly the same, role structures associated with them. Thus the role structure 26 is the same as that of a considerable number of other verbs similar in meaning to *strike*, for example, *hit*, *touch*, and *bump*, all of which may be called verbs of contact. Other verbs of contact must be given somewhat different role-structure representation, however; for example, *beat* must be represented:

27. *beat*: Agent, Instrument, Patient/Location

since a sentence such as:

28. John beat the rug.

is unambiguous, unlike 20. *Collide* must be represented:

29. *collide*: ⟨Patient⟩

since in a sentence like:

30. The train collided with the bus.

the nominal expressions *the train* and *the bus* can only be thought of as patients. Moreover, a sentence such as:

31. *The conductor collided the train with the bus.

is ungrammatical.

Example 31 illustrates what happens when a sentence is formed out of a deep structure that violates the role-structure requirements of a particular predicate. The ungrammaticality is of both a semantic and a syntactic sort. Example 31 is badly formed semantically, because *collide* as ordinarily used in standard English does not make sense when used with an agent, a patient/location, and an instrument (it is easy, however, to extend its meaning so that 31 would be semantically well formed). It is also unsyntactic, because certain of the transformational rules that create subjects and objects are forced through on a predicate that does not permit their application (in particular, *collide* cannot occur with a direct object). Chomsky has coined the term strict subcategorizational restriction to cover such cases; we, however, shall simply call them violations of role structure.

We are now in a position to state the transformational

rules that create the subject, direct object, and oblique object of the verb *strike*. As it turns out, these rules are much more general than that, and are applicable to sentences containing many different sorts of predicates; we therefore state them without reference to any particular predicate.

(a) If an agent is expressed in surface structure, it must become the subject.

(b) If an agent is not expressed, and an instrument is, instrument must become the subject.

(c) If neither agent nor instrument is expressed, then patient/location must become the subject.

(d) If instrument is not the subject, it becomes an oblique object introduced by the preposition *with*.

(e) If patient/location is not the subject, it becomes the direct object.

(f) If a set of two patients is chosen, one of these becomes the subject and the other the direct object (or, as in the case of *collide*, the other patient becomes an oblique object introduced by the preposition *with*).

Rules *a–e* are appropriate to sentences containing at most one agent, patient/location, or instrument; rule *f* is appropriate to those containing a set of two patients. There is another rule that may be applied instead of *f*, according to which all the patients together become the subject, as in the sentences:

32. The hammer and the nail struck.
33. The train and the bus collided.

The rule may be expressed as follows:

(g) If a set of two or more patients is expressed, they may all become the subject, being connected by a coordinate conjunction *and*; or a plural nominal expression may be used.

The last provision in rule *g* is necessary to permit the generation of such sentences as 34 below, while disallowing such sentences as 35:

34. The trains collided.
35. *The train collided.

When three or more patients of the set are expressed, at least one of them must be made the subject:

36. The car, the bus, and the truck collided.
37. The car and the bus collided with the truck.
38. The car collided with the bus and the truck.

4. Other Examples of Role Structures

Let us now turn our attention to another class of predicates which have different role structures—verbs that express changes of state, such as *break*:

39. The boy broke the window [into pieces] with the bat.
40. The boy broke the window [into pieces].
41. The bat broke the window [into pieces].
42. The window broke [into pieces].

The expression *into pieces* has been put in brackets in 39–42 to indicate that these sentences are grammatical with or without such an expression in surface structure. In these examples, *the boy* plays the role of agent, *the window* that of patient (note: not patient/location), *pieces* is result, and *the bat* is instrument.

Example 39 shows that *break* can occur with all four roles. From 40, we learn that if the instrument is not expressed, but the agent is, then the instrument is understood, since the boy must have used something to break the window. From 41, however, we learn that if the instrument is expressed but the agent is not, it is not necessarily the case that the agent is understood (that is, present in deep structure, but absent in surface structure), since 41 can be interpreted in such a way that no agency is involved. Example 42 shows, furthermore, that if neither agent nor instrument are expressed, neither is present in the deep structure. Finally, we observe that result, if not expressed, is always understood. We summarize these findings by assigning to *break* the role structure in 43:

43. *break*: Patient, Result, [Instrument, (Agent)]

The enclosures in 43 indicate that the items within them may, but need not, be chosen. Thus, 43 is an abbreviation for each of the following role structures:

44. *break*: Patient, Result, Instrument, Agent
45. *break*: Patient, Result, Instrument
46. *break*: Patient, Result

The rules for creating subjects and objects of the predicate *break* are the same as those for *strike*, with two exceptions: for "patient/location" read "patient," and a rule relating to result must be added.

(h) If result is expressed, it becomes an oblique object introduced by the preposition *to*, *into*, or *in*.

According to traditional grammar, *break* is used as a causative verb in 39–41 and to designate a simple change of state in 42. The underlying resulting state is indicated by the past participle *broken*, as in the sentence:

47. The window is broken [into pieces].

Other verbs which have the same role structure as *break* include *bend*, *snap*, *rip*, *tear*, *grow*, *shrink*, *crack*, *crumple*, *burn*, *heat*, *warm*, *cool*, *chill*, *freeze*, *solidify*, *liquefy*, and *melt*. Still other verbs, such as *cut* and *erase*, which are similar to these in meaning, can only be used causatively; that is, they have the following role structure:

48. *cut*: Patient, Result, Instrument, (Agent)

Thus, while one can say:

49. The boy cut the cloth with the scissors.
50. The scissors cut the cloth.

the sentence:

51. *The cloth cut.

is ungrammatical.

Finally, there are change-of-state verbs that cannot be used causatively, or that can be used causatively when accompanied by instrument expressions but not by agent expressions. Examples of the first type include *rise* and *vanish*. Thus, one can say:

52. The rabbit vanished.

whereas the following are ungrammatical:

53. *The magician vanished the rabbit [with his wand].
54. *The wand vanished the rabbit.

Examples of the second type include *rot* and *mature*. One can, for example, say:

55. The timbers rotted.
56. Water rotted the timbers.

but not:

57. *John rotted the timbers [with water].

The fact that agents cannot be used with verbs such as *rot* and *mature* suggests that the expression in 56 which we have designated instrument, *water*, should be analyzed as playing a somewhat different role, perhaps that of cause. We shall have more to say on the cause/instrument distinction below. Ignoring this distinction for the present, however, we say that verbs like *vanish* and *rot* have role structures like the following:

58. *vanish*: Patient, Result
59. *rot*: Patient, Result, (Instrument)

It has long been known that certain pairs of verbs have complementary role structures. In the pair *rise* and *raise*, for example, the first can only be used to express a change of state, and the second can only be used causatively. Together, the two verbs have the role structure of the single verb *break*. A particularly interesting pair of verbs with complementary role structures are *kill* and *die*. The verb *kill* can only be used causatively, as the following examples illustrate:

60. John killed the bug with DDT.
61. DDT killed the bug.
62. *The bug killed.

The role of agent is expressed by *John*, that of instrument by *DDT*, and that of patient by *the bug*. The verb *die* can only be used noncausatively:

63. *John died the bug with DDT.
64. *DDT died the bug.
65. The bug died.

Die, however, can be used together with another nominal expression, which plays the role of specifying the cause of death, as in:

66. The victim died of/from loss of blood.

The expression *loss of blood* in 66 certainly cannot be taken to express the instrument role, since no agent can use loss of blood to kill anyone; it would be odd to say:

67. John killed the victim with loss of blood.

It will be noted also that expressions designating cause, like those designating instrument, can be used as the subject of *kill*, as in:

68. Loss of blood killed the victim.

This observation leads us to inquire whether any instrument-like expression, when used in a sentence without an understood agent, is to be taken to designate cause rather than instrument. The answer to this question depends upon whether one takes a sentence such as:

69. Poison killed the victim.

to be ambiguous, and that depends upon whether one assigns the role instrument or cause to the expression *poison*—note that one can say both:

70. The victim died of poison.
71. John killed the victim with poison.

I do think that 69 is ambiguous in this way, from which we conclude that wherever we have included the specification:

72. Instrument, (Agent)

in role structures (as in 43 and 49), it should be replaced by:

73. $\begin{Bmatrix} \text{Instrument, Agent} \\ \text{Cause} \end{Bmatrix}$

The role structure for the verb *kill*, therefore, should be given as:

74. *kill*: Patient, Result, $\begin{Bmatrix} \text{Instrument, Agent} \\ \text{Cause} \end{Bmatrix}$

whereas that of *die* is:

75. *die*: Patient, Result, (Cause)

The role structure of *rot* (given above in 59), moreover, should be revised so as to look like that of *die*.

It will be noted that the transformational rules for making subjects and objects, when applied to *kill* and *die*, operate differently with respect to the role of cause. In the case of *kill*, cause is made subject and patient is made direct object; in the case of *die*, patient is made subject and cause is expressed as an oblique object with either the preposition *of* or *from*.

It was noted earlier that simply to express that a patient is in a particular state, one may use the past participle of a change-of-state verb, for example, *broken*. Such past participles can be viewed as adjectives in their own right, with their own role structures. For example:

76. *broken*: Patient, Result

The difference semantically between a stative past participle such as *broken* and a change-of-state verb such as *vanish*, which happens to have the same role structure (compare 58), is that the participle expresses that the patient is in the state designated by the result, whereas the verb expresses that the patient has come to be in that state. There are, of course, stative adjectives in English that do not happen to be past participles (*hot* as opposed to *heated*, *ripe* as opposed to *ripened*, *rotten* as opposed to *rotted*). There is also, however, a subtle semantic difference between stative adjectives and past participles. The ordinary adjective typically indicates simply that the patient is in a particular state, whereas the past participle typically indicates that the patient has been at some time in a different state, or that the state it is in is being compared with a different state. Thus one says:

77. The soup is hot.

to indicate that the temperature of the soup is above a certain point (appropriate for soup) and nothing more, whereas when one says:

78. The soup is heated.

it is asserted that the temperature of the soup is now higher than at some earlier time. As a result, neither sentence necessarily implies the other; 77 can be affirmed, for example, of soup that never was at a different temperature (for example, of soup made by pouring boiling water over a prepared dry soup mix), and 78 can be affirmed of lukewarm soup that had previously been sitting in the refrigerator. We account for this distinction by positing that stative adjectives like *hot* occur with the roles patient and state rather than with patient and result.

It is worth noticing that sentences containing the causative or change-of-state verb *heat*, for example:

79. The soup heated.
80. John heated the soup.

may always be paraphrased by complex sentences in which the most deeply embedded clause contains the past participle *heated*. Thus 79 has the following paraphrase:

81. The soup came to be heated.

and 80 has the paraphrase:

82. John caused the soup to come to be heated.

Examples 83 and 84 below, however, are not paraphrases of 79 and 80, since 79 and 80 make no claim about the resulting temperature of the soup whereas 83 and 84 do:

83. The soup came to be hot.
84. John caused the soup to come to be hot.

In general, we may say that the meaning of any change-of-state verb *V* is the same as that of *come to be V-ed* where *V-ed* is the past participle of *V*, and the meaning of any causative verb *V* is the same as that of *cause to come to be V-ed*.

An interesting class of change-of-state and causative verbs has to do with motion, for example, the verbs *rise* and *raise* mentioned above. Such verbs may occur with a bewildering array of different expressions of result, provided they express that the patient is at a higher elevation or has a greater quantity than before. The following are a few typical sentences making use of the verb *rise*; the various result expressions have been italicized:

85. The balloon rose *from the floor to the ceiling.*
86. The balloon rose *off the floor.*
87. The balloon rose *twenty feet.*
88. John rose *to his feet.*
89. John's income rose *$100.*

To make precise in the role-structure specifications for verbs like *rise* that its result has to do with upward movement, we use the notation:

90. Result: Movement up

The role structure for *rise* is then:

91. *rise*: Patient, Result: Movement up

The role structure for its causative counterpart *raise* is:

92. *raise*: Patient, Result: Movement up, $\begin{Bmatrix} \text{Agent, Instrument} \\ \text{Cause} \end{Bmatrix}$

Other verbs of motion, for example *descend*, will have different specifications for result. The role structure for *descend*, which is used to indicate change of state (the role of location specifies the surface on which the descent takes place), is:

93. *descend*: Patient, Result: Movement down, (Location)

Still other verbs of motion do not specify the direction of movement, in which case the specification for result will not indicate any particular direction. Such is the case with the verb *move*, the role structure of which is:

94. *move*: Patient, Result: Movement, (Location), $\left(\begin{Bmatrix} \text{Agent, Instrument} \\ \text{Cause} \end{Bmatrix} \right)$

While the expressions of result that are used with motion verbs such as *rise*, *descend*, and *move* have to do with movement, those that are used with motion verbs such as *lay*, *put*, and *place* have to do with the resulting location of the patient. In the sentence:

95. John laid the magazine on the coffee table.

we identify *John* as agent, *the magazine* as patient, and *the coffee table* as result: location on. Corresponding to the causative verb *lay*, in standard English, is the stative verb *lie*, the role structure of which is simply:

96. *lie*: Patient, Location on

The verb *put*, like *lay*, is a causative verb, but its result expression is not specified for any particular type of location. If we ask now what stative verb corresponds to *put* in the manner in which *lie* corresponds to *lay*, we discover that it is the verb *be*. To see this, compare the sentences:

97. John put the car in the garage.
98. The car is in the garage.

with:

95. John laid the magazine on the coffee table.
99. The magazine lay on the coffee table.

Thus, *be* is a stative verb and hence the main predicate in a sentence such as 98, whereas it is not a predicate at all when it is followed by an adjective or a predicate noun, as in examples 1 and 8 of Chapter 3.

The discussion of roles and role structures in this and in the preceding section only begins to scratch the surface of the problem of determining what the linguistically significant roles are in English, and of providing a role-structure analysis of English predicates. Eventually, it will be necessary for linguistic theory to come up with a universal inventory of roles and a statement of how they may be combined into role structures, but at the moment we are nowhere near achieving such goals. (See items 18–32 at the end of this chapter for further discussion.)

5. Deletion of Roles

As we have already noted, sometimes roles appear in deep structures which do not appear in the corresponding surface structures. Other roles, however, must appear in surface structures if they appear at all in the corresponding deep structures. Typically, the roles that may be deleted are precisely those whose lexical content is the most probable, given the meaning of the predicate. Thus, although the result role is required in the deep structures of all sentences whose main predicate is the change-of-state verb *die*, it is rarely expressed in the surface structures of these sentences. The reason is that the result of *die* is typically expressed by the noun *death*, and although it is all right to say something like:

100. The bug died a death.

it is much more natural to express the deep structure underlying 100 by 65:

65. The bug died.

In fact, result is rarely expressed at all, regardless of the main verb, unless there is something special about the result that one wishes to communicate, as in:

101. The bug died a particularly gruesome death.
102. The window broke into thousands of tiny, jagged pieces.

Certain verbs of contact are associated with particular instruments, and again, unless one wishes to say something special about those instruments, they are not expressed in surface structures. Associated with *kick* is the instrument *the foot*; with *kiss*, *the lips*; with *wink*, *the eyelids*; with *slap*, *the (flat of the) hand*; with *punch*, *the fist*; with *embrace*, *the arms*; and so forth. Thus, in the absence of anything special to say about the instrument being used, we might say:

103. Maude kicked Melinda.

If there were something special to say about it, we might say something like:

104. Maude kicked Melinda with her left foot.

The verb *shave* is associated both with the instrument *the razor*, and with the patient/location *the face* (or *the beard*), and normally, both instrument and patient/location are deleted, as in:

105. John is shaving.

But one does not have to use a razor, nor does one have to do it on the face, for we can also say:

106. John is shaving a peach with a rusty knife.

Verbs of consumption such as *eat*, *drink*, and *smoke* are associated with particular patients, which are often deleted; if we say:

107. John is eating.

we understand that he is eating food, probably at a meal. If there is something special about what he is eating, then of course the patient is expressed, as in:

108. John is eating fried earthworms.

Curiously, the typically deleted patient of the verb *drink* generally refers not simply to liquid, but to alcoholic beverage, and when the patient is not expressed, the verb *smoke* is assumed to occur with any form of burning tobacco (there may, however, exist subcultures where different assumptions are made).

On the other hand, there is a handful of verbs in English that have very fussy requirements about what can occur as patient in connection with them, and yet the patient cannot be deleted. One such verb is *stub*; one can only stub one's toes or fingers. Nevertheless, we say:

109. I stubbed my toe.
110. I stubbed my finger.

and not:

111. *I stubbed.

If we now consider a sentence such as:

112. The carpenter hammered the nail into the board.

we might be tempted to obtain it transformationally from the deep structure that also underlies:

113. The carpenter drove the nail into the board with a hammer.

Such a transformation would replace the predicate *drive* by the noun that occurs as its instrument in 113. This proposal will not work however, since 112 and 113 are not stylistic variants. Sentence 112 suggests, but does not claim, that the carpenter used an actual hammer to drive the nail, whereas of course 113 makes such a claim outright. The correct interpretation of 112 is that the carpenter used something in a hammer-like fashion to drive the nail into the board. This is borne out by the fact that we can use expressions other than *a hammer* as instruments in connection with the verb *hammer*, as in:

114. The carpenter hammered the nail into the board with his shoe.

Therefore, 112 is not to be derived transformationally from any deep structure like that underlying 113, but rather directly from a deep structure in which the main predicate is *hammer* and in which the instrument is expressed by something like *an object which can be used as a hammer* (which of course is most likely to actually be a hammer). The meaning of the verb *hammer* is "drive in a hammerlike fashion," which explains that it takes on the same role structure as the verb *drive*, just as causative verbs generally have the role structure of *cause*. Many other nouns that name carpentry tools may be used as verbs in ways analogous to *hammer*.

As further evidence that verbs such as *hammer* are not to be transformationally derived from their use as instrumental nouns, consider the sentence:

115. John is sawing his meat.

In this case, the deleted instrument is quite clearly *a knife*, and not *a saw*, and what the sentence asserts is the same as that asserted by:

116. John is cutting his meat with a knife in a sawlike fashion.

Given the existence of these denominal verbs, it is usually easy to determine the verbal sense that is basic to their meanings. With *hammer*, we associate the verb *drive*; with *saw*, the verb *cut*; with *nail*, the verb *hang* or *attach*; with *net*, the verb *catch*. There are, however, a few slight surprises. Consider for example:

117. A hoodlum knifed me.

Clearly, the sense of the verb *knife* is "stab with a knife-like object," yet a priori we might have assumed that the verb *knife* would have meant "cut with a knifelike object." Ambiguities can also arise; consider for example:

118. The Smiths are air-conditioning their bedroom.

To me, this can mean either 119 or 120 below:

119. The Smiths are cooling their bedroom with an air-conditioner.

120. The Smiths are installing an air-conditioner in their bedroom.

It is possible for two different predicates with the same role structure to differ with respect to how their roles are expressed and, therefore, which of their roles can be deleted. The verbs *rob* and *steal* are excellent examples. Both verbs can be said to have the following role structure, in which source designates the person or institution affected:

121. Agent, Patient, Source

Thus, we have such sentences as:

122. A masked bandit stole $5,000 from the bank.
123. A masked bandit robbed the bank of $5,000.

With the predicate *steal*, the expression designating the source may be deleted, whereas with *rob*, the patient may be deleted:

124. A masked bandit stole $5,000.
125. A masked bandit robbed the bank.

6. The Analysis of Prepositions

From the examples considered so far in this chapter, we observe that the choice of preposition corresponds closely to the role played by the nominal expression following it. The preposition *with* very often introduces the instrument, *from* typically introduces with source, *to* the goal, and *to*, *into*, or *in* the result. The absence of a preposition before a nominal expression indicates something only of its syntactic function in the sentence—it is either subject or direct object. The expression designating the agent never occurs in a core sentence with a preposition because, if the expression is present, it is always made the subject of the sentence. In a passive sentence, however, as we saw in Chapter 3, Section 3, the agent expression becomes an oblique object introduced by the preposition *by*. It seems reasonable, therefore, to assume that every role in deep structures of English sentences is accompanied by a preposition of its own, and that this preposition is deleted if the role is made into the subject or direct object of the sentence.

In many cases, it is clear that whether a particular role is made into a direct or oblique object depends rather idiosyncratically on the main verb. For example, when we compare the sentences:

126. Annette arrived at the hotel.
127. Annette reached the hotel.
128. Annette made it to the hotel.

we conclude, as a first approximation to the truth, that the role structures of *arrive*, *reach*, and *make it* are the same, namely:

129. Patient, Result: Location at

The three verbs differ only syntactically, in that the expression designating result becomes the direct object of *reach* but an oblique object of *arrive* and *make it*, with the preposition *at* and *to* respectively. Many other examples of a similar sort could also be given (see item 30 at the end of this chapter).

Unlike verbs, predicate adjectives and nouns do not occur with direct objects in English, so that except for the subject, every role in an adjectival or nominal sentence is introduced by a preposition. As a result, one can easily find adjectives and verbs, and nouns and verbs, of similar meaning; the verb occurs with a direct object, and the adjective or noun with an oblique object. Compare, for example:

130. The mechanic is aware of the difficulty.
131. The mechanic recognizes the difficulty.

and, on the other hand:

132. Sarah was the mother of Abraham.
133. Sarah bore Abraham.

The oblique object of a predicate noun can, moreover, be converted transformationally into a prenominal genitive expression (see Chapter 3, item 2), so that 132 has as a stylistic variant:

134. Sarah was Abraham's mother.

Also, as example 9 of Chapter 3 illustrates, a subordinate clause that functions to express a role of a predicate is never introduced by a preposition, even if that predicate happens to be an adjective. Consequently, we assume that there is an obligatory transformation which deletes any preposition that precedes such a subordinate clause. The existence of this rule is confirmed by the observation that when a sentence with a subject clause is made passive, no preposition appears in front of that clause in the passive sentence. Thus:

135. You annoy John.

136. John is annoyed *by* you.

but:

137. That he has to stay after school annoys John.
138. John is annoyed that he has to stay after school.

Also compare:

139. I persuaded John *of* his need to lose weight.
140. I persuaded John that he needed to lose weight.

and:

141. I insist *on* your taking me to a nice restaurant.
142. I insist that you take me to a nice restaurant.

With these facts regarding the transformational deletion of prepositions in mind, let us attempt a somewhat more thorough correlation of prepositions with the roles of the nominal expressions that they introduce. This is provided in the following table.

Correlation of Roles with Prepositions

ROLE	PREPOSITION
Agent	by
Patient	of, to
Instrument	with, by
Cause	by
Result	to, in, into
Stimulus	of, to, by
Source	from
Goal	to
Location	in, at, on, near, around, beyond, . . .
Movement	into, onto, to, toward, from, through, across, . . .

A glance at the table reveals that the same role may be introduced by a variety of prepositions, and that the same preposition may be used to introduce many different roles.

Instrument is introduced by *with*, and possibly also by *by* or *through*, while the preposition *by* may be used to introduce agent, location by, or instrument. That location and movement may be subdivided into such roles as location in, location at, location by, movement to (which perhaps is to be identified as the same role we have called goal), movement from (perhaps to be identified with source), movement around, movement through, suggests that the prepositions indicating location and movement are to be taken as predicates in their own right (see item 34 for an elaboration of this possibility).

As we have seen, some predicates, for example *move* and *put*, may be used with any movement or location expression, whereas others, for example *rise* and *lay*, may only be used with particular movement and location expressions. The choice of particular location- or movement-designating prepositions is not entirely fixed, even in the latter cases, by the main predicate. The choice may also depend on the nominal expression following. Consider, for example:

143. I live in Conshohocken, Pennsylvania.
144. I live on the east side of town.
145. I live at 77 Massachusetts Avenue.

That *in* is used in 143, *on* in 144, and *at* in 145 has nothing to do with the verb *live*, but rather with what the following nominal expression designates (roughly, one lives *in* cities, towns, and countries; one lives *on* particular streets or parts of town; and one lives *at* a particular address).

A more careful analysis will also force us to make a distinction between the roles location or movement in space and location or movement in time, for there are some predicates that require the use of temporal roles only, or of spatial roles only. If we compare the sentences:

146. The delegate walked into the auditorium.
147. The meeting lasted into the morning.

we recognize that the predicate *walk* occurs only with the

role movement in space, while *last* is used only with movement in time. The fact that we can say both:

148. John drove into the gas station.
149. John drove into the night.

does not mean that the predicate *drive* can be used with either movement-in-time roles or movement-in-space roles. Rather, it occurs with movement in space, which may be deleted transformationally, and it occurs optionally with a role which we may call duration in time, which is normally introduced by the prepositions *for* or *into*. By a curious, but not illogical habit, we measure time duration either in temporal or spatial units. If one drives at a constant speed of 60 miles per hour, one can say with equal truthfulness:

150. I drove for three hours.
151. I drove for 180 miles.

Here the expressions *three hours* and *180 miles* both denote duration in time.

As noted earlier in this chapter, we have not exhausted the list of possible roles in our discussion, and indeed the question how many roles will have to be distinguished in English grammar—and, more important, in universal grammar—has by no means been answered. Even the question whether there is any firm upper limit on the number of such roles has not been settled. We have, however, given an account of a considerable number of the important ones, and of how they are to be dealt with in both semantics and syntax. Some consideration of roles other than those discussed above is to be found in the problems and questions that follow.

PROBLEMS AND
SUGGESTIONS FOR
FURTHER STUDY

1. Just as Robert Lees's *The Grammar of English Nomi-nalizations* represents the most significant effort to apply early generative-transformational theory to significant problems in English syntax, so Peter S. Rosenbaum's *The Grammar of English Predicate Complement Constructions* embodies the most thorough application of later generative-transformational theory to such problems. Both books also originated as doctoral dissertations written under Chomsky's direction. For a general introduction to later generative-transformational theory, see Peter S. Rosenbaum and Roderick Jacobs, *English Transformational Grammar*; D. Terence Langendoen, *The Study of Syntax*, chapters 1–5; and Noam Chomsky, "The Formal Nature of Language," Appendix A to Eric Lenneberg, *The Biological Foundations of Language*, pages 397–442.

2. The ideas in Katz and Fodor's pioneering article on

semantics have been further elaborated and developed in a number of articles and books by Katz. See in particular Katz's articles in Fodor and Katz (eds.), *The Structure of Language*, and his book *The Philosophy of Language*. For a somewhat different approach to the relation of syntax to semantics, see Uriel Weinreich, "Explorations in Semantic Theory," in Thomas A. Sebeok (ed.), *Current Trends in Linguistics*, Vol. 3, *Theoretical Foundations*; also see McCawley's review of this book. Katz's reply to Weinreich is contained in his article "Recent Issues in Semantic Theory." Katz's views are further criticized in James McCawley, "The Role of Semantics in Grammar," in Emmon Bach and Robert Harms (eds.), *Universals in Linguistic Theory*.

3. The analysis of roles and role structures presented in this chapter is based largely on the work of Charles J. Fillmore. See his "The Case for Case," in *Universals in Linguistic Theory*; "Lexical Entries for Verbs"; and "Review of Bendix, *Componential Analysis of General Vocabulary*." There are certain terminological differences between Fillmore's account and the one given here. Our "notion role" corresponds to Fillmore's "case," and our "role structure" corresponds to his "case frame."

4. Fillmore's ideas concerning the nature of assumptions (Fillmore calls them presuppositions) are developed in the latter two articles cited in item 3. See also James McCawley, "Concerning the Base Component of a Transformational Grammar."

5. How do the verbs *murder* and *assassinate* differ from *kill* in the assumptions they make concerning the entities that express the agent and patient roles used with these verbs?

6. The notion that a sentence can be viewed as a miniature drama, complete with plot and roles, is suggested in Robert Longacre, *Grammar Discovery Procedures*. Fill-

more has also suggested that scenarios like the following might be useful in teaching roles and role structure to children. A boy (patient) walks onto an empty stage and falls down. This illustrates the role structure of the verb *trip* in such sentences as:

152. The boy tripped.

In the next scene, a boy is standing on an otherwise empty stage, and suddenly a cane (cause) appears, tripping the boy, and causing him to fall down. This illustrates the role structure of *trip* in such sentences as:

153. The cane tripped the boy.

Next a boy and a girl are standing on an otherwise empty stage, and suddenly the girl (agent) takes a cane (instrument) and uses it to trip the boy, causing him to fall down. This illustrates the role structure of *trip* in such sentences as:

154. The girl tripped the boy with a cane.

7. The ambiguity of the sentence:

155. Strangers frighten my dog.

can be accounted for by postulating that the subject *strangers* can be interpreted as playing either of two different roles. What are they? What is the role structure of the predicate *frighten*?

8. Also give the role structures of the predicates *fear* (verb), *afraid* (adjective) and *frightening* (adjective). What rules for selecting subjects and objects does each obey?

9. On the basis of examples 5–12, formulate rules to govern the selection of subject and object for the roles patient, stimulus, and observation. Obviously, different predicates make use of different rules. Is there any subtle difference in meaning between the predicates that make the patient

the subject, and those that make the stimulus or observation the subject?

10. Notice that although the sentence:

    156. John hit the windshield.

    is ambiguous (for reasons given in the text in connection with example 20), the following sentence is unambiguous:

    157. John hit himself.

    Why is this? Hint—notice that 158 does not make sense:

    158. John collided with himself.

11. The sentence:

    159. John hit the ceiling.

    has, besides its two literal interpretations parallel to those of 156, a third interpretation, roughly:

    160. John manifested great anger.

    We refer to this third interpretation as its idiomatic meaning. How should the idiomatic meaning of 159 be accounted for? Hint—notice that 156 does not have an idiomatic meaning, nor do:

    161. John hit the ceiling of his girl friend's one-room efficiency in The Bronx.
    162. The ceiling was hit by John.
    163. Whose ceiling did John hit?

12. Give examples of sentences using the predicate *strike* which are ungrammatical because they manifest violations of role structure. Why is it often arguable whether a particular sentence manifests such a violation?

13. Any given predicate is likely to have a variety of meanings. For example, besides "come into sharp contact," *strike* can mean "encounter by digging," "light," and "refuse to take up one's job," as in:

164. The men struck oil.
165. The men struck matches.
166. The men struck the company warehouse.

Obviously, each use of the predicate makes different assumptions about what may fulfill its roles; do these various uses also have different role structures? Why is it difficult to determine whether one is dealing with a single predicate with different meanings (a polyseme), or several predicates, each with its own meaning (homonyms)?

14. Compare the sentences:

167. The chair slid across the room.
168. John slid across the room.

Account for the ambiguity of 168 and the unambiguity of 167 in terms of the roles which *the chair* and *John* can play as subjects of the predicate *slide*.

15. A set of different forms which together cover the ground normally taken care of by a single form is called a suppletive set. Examples include *person, people; am, are;* and pairs of verbs such as *rise, raise; lie, lay.* There is a certain arbitrariness, however, in deciding which verbs are to be paired as suppletives (a case could be made for considering *elevate* or *heighten* the causative counterpart to *rise*). Are there, then, other criteria besides simple complementarity that can be used to determine suppletive pairs? This problem has plagued linguists for a long time; see, for example, Bernard Bloch and George L. Trager, *Outline of Linguistic Analysis*.

16. Examples 81 and 82 were called paraphrases of 79 and 80, rather than stylistic variants, because the paired sentences do not mean exactly the same thing. For example, 82 could be used to describe a situation in which John, as a customer at a restaurant, complained that the soup was too cold, so that the waiter returned it to the kitchen

to be heated; whereas 80 could not be so used. Thus, we should say that the meaning of a causative verb *V* is the same as that of *directly cause to come to be V-ed.* For an insightful discussion of the syntax and semantics of change-of-state and causative verbs, see George Lakoff, *On the Nature of Syntactic Irregularity*, Appendix F. Some of Lakoff's ideas are also discussed in my *Study of Syntax*, Chapter 6. Also see Fillmore, "The Case for Case," for an alternative to Lakoff's approach.

17. There is often a clear relationship between the written or spoken form of certain stative adjectives, and change-of-state and causative verbs. Linguists speak of these as morphological relationships (morphology is the study of the makeup of stems, suffixes, and prefixes—how they are built up out of units of speech—and of how these elements are combined to form words). In some cases the adjective and verb are identical, (*cool, warm, yellow*). In a few cases, the verb is differentiated from the adjective by a change in vowel (*hot* versus *heat*). In many cases, the verb is formed by the addition of the suffix *-en* to the adjective (*ripe, ripen; soft, soften; wide, widen; black, blacken*). In others, the suffix *-ify* is added to form the verb, perhaps with other changes (*solid, solidify; liquid, liquefy*). In still others, an archaic past participle has been made over into a purely stative adjective (*dead, open, swollen, molten*). Make a list of change-of-state verbs formed with *-en*, and see if you can determine any phonological properties that the underlying adjectives have in common. What do you make of the forms *enlarge, enrich, empower*? Of the relationship of *rotten* to *rot*? Of *worsen*? What are some common adjectives which have no morphologically related change-of-state or causative verb? Extend the sense of suppletion given in item 15 to cover the relationship of the adjective *good* to the change-of-state and causative verb *improve*.

18. Consider the class of verbs that may be called maintenance-of-state verbs, such as *hold, survive, resist, withstand,* and *maintain.* Which of these verbs can be used causatively and which cannot? Consider the sentence:

> 169. The settlers held Fort Necessity against the Indians with fifty guns.

Under the interpretation that it was the settlers who had fifty guns, we can identify *the settlers* as agent, *Fort Necessity* as patient, and *fifty guns* as instrument. What role would you suggest for the *Indians?* Similarly, in the sentence:

> 170. The retaining wall withstood the force of the waves.

what role would you assign to *the force of the waves?*

19. What role would you suggest for the expression *this boulder* in the following sentence:

> 171. This boulder informs us that the ice-age glacier must have reached at least this far south.

20. In the following sentence, the two italicized finite clauses play different roles:

> 172. *That John was rude to his teacher* proves *that he has no respect for his elders.*

What suggestions do you have for identifying what they are? This question is taken up somewhat by Fillmore in "The Case for Case." Give some other verbs which, like *prove,* can be used with clauses as subject and object. What role structures do these verbs have? Consider also such sentences as:

> 173. That John was rude to his teacher proves to me that he has no respect for his elders.
> 174. Harry proved to me that John has no respect for his elders.

175. Harry proved that John has no respect for his elders.

21. In the examples we have considered in the text, the expressions used to indicate roles have always been nominal expressions. But adverbial expressions can also be used to indicate roles. Consider the sentences:

    176. The balloon rose to the ceiling.
    177. The balloon rose five feet.
    178. The balloon rose a little bit.
    179. The balloon rose slightly.

    Why is *slightly* in 179 to be considered an expression of the result role associated with *rise*? Give other examples that illustrate the use of adverbial expressions to indicate roles.

22. With some predicates, in fact, it is normal for a particular role to be expressed adverbially, the use of nominal expressions being highly constrained. Show that this is the case with the result role associated with the predicate *frighten*.

23. Compare the sentences:

    180. The driver loaded furniture onto the truck.
    181. The driver loaded the truck with furniture.

    How do these sentences differ in meaning? What would you identify as the roles of the various nominal expressions in them? Show that the properties of these sentences can be accounted for by assuming that *load* in 181 means "fill by loading." Similarly, compare the sentences:

    182. The child smeared crayon on the wall.
    183. The child smeared the wall with crayon.

    How would you analyze the meaning of *smear* in 183? For further discussion of predicates of this sort, see Fillmore, "Lexical Entries for Verbs."

24. Give examples showing that one does not normally say anything special about the result role associated with the verb *kill*, and that it is therefore generally deleted in core sentences in which *kill* is the main predicate.

25. What roles would you assign to the expressions *my husband* and *fifteen dollars* in the sentence:

    184. I bought a pipe for my husband for fifteen dollars.

    Give other sentences with different predicates in which one or the other or both of these roles are used. Notice that *for my husband* may be moved next to the verb by the indirect-object-movement transformation discussed in Chapter 3. Give other examples (using different main predicates) in which this transformation is applicable to nominal expressions introduced by the preposition *for*.

26. What role is being played by *you* in the following sentence:

    185. I told your mother on you.

    Feel free to name it anything which strikes you as appropriate, since as far as I know, no grammarian has ever given it a name in English. With what sorts of verbs is the role characteristically used? Why is it more "natural" to say 186 than 187:

    186. John walked out on me.
    187. John left on me.

    How would you explain the unnaturalness of the sentences:

    188. Sylvia married Harry's rival on him.
    189. The surgeon left a sponge in Harry on him.

27. What roles are being played by *Mary* in the following two sentences? Can they be identified with any of the roles discussed in the text or in problems 25 and 26?

190. What I did for Mary was give her a C.
191. What I did to Mary was give her a C.

Compare also:

192. I did something nice for Mary.
193. I did something nasty to Mary.

28. Show that although the verb *climb* may be used with any movement result, movement up is the only role that can be deleted in sentences in which *climb* is the main predicate.

29. Account for the ambiguity of the sentence:

   194. The maid is dusting the plant.

   Can you think of verbs other than *dust* that can be used ambiguously in this way? Similarly, account for the ambiguity of:

   195. John is stringing the beans.

30. Show that in some cases, whether an object will be oblique or direct depends on whether or not the verb has a prefix of some sort. As a start, consider the sentences:

   196. John lives in a dingy apartment.
   197. John inhabits a dingy apartment.
   198. Magellan sailed around the world.
   199. Magellan circumnavigated the world.

31. What does each of the following mean when it is used as a verb: *sail, canoe, jet, motor, cycle, motorcycle?* Can an argument be made that these verbs are transformationally related to instrumental nouns?

32. Using the apparatus developed in this chapter and in these items, account for as many of the senses of the following sentence as you can (I have been able to come up with four quite distinct interpretations, so far):

200. John flew to Miami.

†33. When a predicate, like *collide*, is used with a set of expressions all of which play the same role, we say that such a predicate is symmetric. By virtue of their respective role structures, *collide* is always symmetric, *hit* may be symmetric, and *beat* is never symmetric. Categorize the following predicates according to whether they must be, may be, or cannot be used symmetrically: *touch, hold, love, marry, kiss, embrace, hug, caress, confer, agree, meet, fight, argue, discuss, debate, attach, join, separate, differ, resemble, similar, equal, brother, sibling, cousin, relative, uncle, friend, enemy, spouse, wife.*

†34. Certain prepositions in English have semantic and syntactic properties resembling those of verbs and adjectives, and for this reason it may be argued that they, too, are fundamentally predicative in nature. A few prepositions can be used directly as verbs, in a different but related sense. Consider, for example:

201. John downed his drink in one gulp.
202. The bank upped its interest rate on savings accounts.

Certain sentences in which a preposition plus nominal expression is used following the supposed main verb *be* (see example 98 and discussion concerning it) may be paraphrased by sentences in which a verb "replaces" *be*-plus-preposition (perhaps also with a change in what becomes subject and object). Consider, for example:

 98. The car is in the garage.
203. The garage contains a car.
204. This poem is about the war.
205. This poem concerns the war.
206. This sonata is by Beethoven.
207. Beethoven wrote/composed this sonata.

208. John's house is near the railroad station.
209. The position of John's house approximates that of the railroad station.

On the basis of such examples, it might be argued that the main predicate in 98 is *in*, and that *the car* and *the garage* have roles in relation to it, rather than to the verb *be*. To see if this proposal has any merit, we need answers to such questions as the following. How general is the ability to paraphrase *be*-plus-preposition by a verb? What additional roles do we need to postulate if prepositions are to be analyzed as predicates? How would the proposal affect the analysis of sentences of the sort we have already considered? For example, what deep structure would we then assign to a sentence such as:

210. John remained in bed.

Would the new analysis of such sentences be superior to the sort of analysis developed in this chapter?

5

THE INTRODUCTION OF NOMINAL EXPRESSIONS

According to both early and later generative-transformational theory, the nominal expressions which serve as subjects and objects of sentences are assumed to be directly introduced as such into the deep structures of the sentences in which they occur. In recent papers (see item 1 at the end of this chapter), Emmon Bach, Paul Postal, and James McCawley have argued, rather, that only the lexical content of predicate nominal expressions should be introduced in the deep structure, while that of other nominal expressions should be introduced transformationally. They have also argued that the places where nouns turn up in surface structures are, in deep structures, occupied by variables, roughly in the manner we described at the end of Chapter 3. In this chapter, we shall explore the nature and ramifications of these claims and present some of the arguments in support of them. Although we shall attempt to keep the presentation as simple as possible, some of the arguments are complicated and involve rather subtle semantic judgments. The reader who is not interested in pursuing the more difficult arguments may without loss of continuity skip sections 4, 5, 6, and 8 below (they are marked with a dagger).

1. Role Structures in Predicate Nominal Sentences

Since we regard predicate nominal expressions as the deep-structure source for all nominal expressions, predicate or non-predicate, we begin by considering some of the properties of sentences in which predicate nominal expressions are used. For simplicity in the following discussion, we shall use the terms "noun" and "nominal expression" interchangeably.

First of all, consider such simple predicate-noun sentences as the following:

1. Ruby is a soprano.
2. Leopold was the king of Belgium.

We say that in 1 the predicate noun *soprano* is a one-place predicate whose subject is *Ruby*, and in 2, *king* is a two-place predicate whose subject is *Leopold* and whose oblique object is *Belgium*. We ask next: What roles are being played by these various subjects and objects?

The role being played by the subjects of 1 and 2 seems to be simply that of identifying the party designated by the predicate noun. This is a role we have not heretofore encountered in our considerations, so we shall make up a name for it—"essive," based on the Latin *esse*, "to be." In general, the subject of a predicate-noun sentence always has the essive role; this is one of the few places in English grammar where semantics and syntax coincide. The role of *Belgium* in 2 has already been encountered; it is patient.

The subject of a predicate noun sentence can simultaneously play other roles besides that of essive. Consider the following:

3. Ruby is a beautiful soprano.
4. Leopold was a good king.

Both sentences 3 and 4 are ambiguous; 3 is paraphrasable as either 5 or 6 below, and 4 is paraphrasable as either 7 or 8 below:

5. Ruby is a beautiful person who is a soprano.
6. Ruby sings soprano beautifully.
7. Leopold was a good person who was a king.
8. Leopold ruled well as king.

In examples 5 and 7, *Ruby* and *Leopold* continue to play just the essive role, but in 6 and 8 it is clear that their roles are that of agent. But then *Ruby* and *Leopold* in sentences 3 and 4, when these are interpreted as 6 and 8, must simultaneously play the essive and agent roles.

Other multiple roles are possible for subjects of predicate nouns. Consider, for example:

9. The Common is a good spot for watching demagogues.
10. The Vice President has been a target of abuse.

In 9, the subject plays the multiple role essive-location. In 10 it plays that of essive-goal. Now consider:

11. Alcohol was Harry's downfall.
12. Harry's downfall was alcohol.

In 11, the subject *alcohol* plays the multiple essive-cause role, but in 12, in which subject and predicate noun have been reversed, the role played by the subject *Harry's downfall* is clearly that of essive-result. In general, in a sentence in which the original subject is essive-cause, interchanging subject and predicate noun creates a sentence in which the subject is essive-result. Compare also the sentences:

13. Air pollution will be man's undoing.
14. Air pollution is man's doing.

In 13, *air pollution* has the role essive-cause, but in 14 it has the role essive-result.

Generally, the identification of the role played by the oblique object of a predicate noun is no problem, as we saw in 2, but important roles are encountered there that we have not yet considered. Take, for example, sentences such as:

15. This is my collection of butterflies.
16. This is part of my collection of butterflies.

The role of *butterflies* in 15 includes that of patient, since here the relationship of *butterflies* to *collection* is similar to that of *butterflies* to the verb *collect* in the sentence:

17. I collect butterflies.

In example 17, the role of *butterflies* is clearly that of patient. But in 15, *butterflies* also specifies the content of the collection; its role in that sentence may therefore be identified as "patient/content." The role of *my collection of butterflies* in 16 is to specify the whole of which *this* is part. We identify the role of this expression, the oblique object of the predicate noun *part*, as "partitive." (For further consideration of these and other roles in predicate-noun sentences, see items 2–7 at the end of this chapter.)

2. The Meaning of Predicate Nouns

The meaning of a predicate noun can be decomposed into two parts—that which is normally assumed about the entities playing roles in connection with it, and that which is normally asserted about those entities. Thus, in a sentence containing the predicate noun *bachelor*, one normally assumes about its essive subject that it is male, human, and adult, and one asserts that it is unmarried. The need for such a distinction becomes apparent when we consider negative predicate-noun sentences, such as:

18. Jackie isn't a bachelor.

Example 18 would normally be used to deny that Jackie is unmarried, but hardly to deny that the entity is male, or is an adult, or is a human being. In general, assumptions remain fixed in negative sentences; only what the affirmative counter-part asserts is denied. To take another example, consider the sentence:

19. Jackie isn't a boy.

Example 19 is subject to different interpretations, depending upon what aspects of the meaning of *boy* are being assumed and what aspects are being denied. One possibility is that it is assumed that Jackie is a male human and that it is denied that he is young (or immature). Another is that it is assumed that Jackie is a young human and that it is denied that Jackie is male.

Such facts as these can be directly accounted for if the meaning of predicate nouns is given in the form of another noun (of more general meaning) plus one or more relative clauses, such that the more general noun (which, however, need not necessarily correspond to an actual word of English) is the embodiment of the assumptions associated with the original noun, and that the relative clause or clauses specify the assertion of the original noun. Thus, we give as the defini-tion of bachelor:

20. *bachelor*: a man who is unmarried

and of *boy*:

21. *boy*: a male human who is young, or a child who is male.

That the definitions of nouns in ordinary dictionaries look very much like the entries given in 20 and 21 can be inter-preted as evidence that the account of the meaning of nouns given here has sound intuitive support.

It will be observed upon examination of the meanings of large numbers of nouns in English that the nouns which ex-press assumptions are very often nouns of quite general mean-ing, such as *man, woman, person, group, thing, substance, device,* or *event.* Particular nouns are often used to make either precise (or technical) assertions or casual ones. This difference is reflected in definitions in which the content of the relative clause is detailed and specific on the one hand, or general and unspecific on the other. Thus, the definition of *bachelor* given in 20 is presumably what is being used in casual, everyday speech, whereas in a technical discussion in which one needs to distinguish between men who are unmarried because they happen to be Roman Catholic priests and men who are unmarried out of choice, one would presumably invest bachelor with something like the meaning given in 22:

22. *bachelor*: a man who is unmarried by choice.

In general, nouns will have a variety of definitions, depending upon the degrees of semantic precision which may be required of them. (For further consideration of these matters, see problems 8–9.)

3. The Introduction of Nonpredicate Nouns

In Bach's paper "Nouns and Noun Phrases," a number of purely syntactic arguments are given for considering that nonpredicate nouns in English should be introduced transformationally. One of these rests on the contention that pairs of sentences like the following are stylistic variants:

23. I met a bachelor at the party.
24. I met someone who was a bachelor at the party.

In example 24, *who was a bachelor* is a relative clause modifying the indefinite pronoun *someone*, and Bach argues that sentences like 24 represent structures that are closer to deep structure than sentences like 23. Sentences like 23 are, in his view, to be derived transformationally by rules which (a) delete a relative pronoun and any inflected form of the verb *be*, and (b) replace an indefinite pronoun such as *someone* or *something* (which function semantically just like variables) by the predicate noun in the underlying relative clause. Bach points out that, after all, rule (*a*) is needed anyway in the

grammar of English, to account for the fact that the following sentences are stylistic variants:

25. I met someone who was intelligent at the party.
26. I met someone intelligent at the party.

The only new thing in his proposal, therefore, is rule (b).
Bach gives a number of semantic arguments to support his
analysis. Perhaps the most important of these has to do with
the fact that entities change their character over time, and
a noun that is appropriate for something at one time is not
necessarily appropriate for it at another. Something that was
a caterpillar some time ago may be a butterfly now; yesterday's baseball player may be today's insurance salesman; and
what is a star today may be a supernova tomorrow. Despite
this, one may truthfully affirm:

27. John's wife was born at home.
28. The rock is now a pile of dust.

and even:

29. Complete this sentence in twenty-five words or less:
    I like Toast Poasties because _____.

What sentence 27 affirms, of course, is that the person who
now is John's wife was born at home, not that she was his
wife when she was born. Sentence 28 does not equate something that is a rock with a pile of dust, but rather something
that was a rock. Finally, in 29, the thing which is to be com-
pleted will not be a sentence until the command is carried
out. That is to say, 27–29 are respectively stylistic variants of:

30. The one who *is* John's wife was born at home.
31. The thing that *was* a rock is now a pile of dust.
32. Complete this thing which *will be* a sentence in twenty-
    five words or less: I like Toast Poasties because _____.

Bach's proposal neatly accounts for the relationship between
these sentences, because rule (a) is formulated so as to delete
a relative pronoun plus any form of the verb *be*, whether it

refers to past, present, or future time, and then rule (*b*) deletes the expression (generally *one* or *thing*) that acts as the variable.

Upon replacing a variable, a predicate noun takes on the role that the variable had in the main clause and the role that the relative pronoun had in the original relative clause. In sentence 33 below, the expression *a beautiful soprano* plays the role of patient of the main verb *meet*, and simultaneously it is interpreted as either essive or essive-agent (that is, the expression may refer either to a beautiful person who is a soprano or a person who sings soprano beautifully):

33. I met a beautiful soprano at the party.

Similarly, in the sentence:

34. The city tore up the Common to build an underground parking garage.

the Common simultaneously expresses the patient of the main verb *tear up*, and essive-location from the underlying relative clause *which was the Common*.

†4. More on the Introduction of Nonpredicate Nouns

If the arguments in the preceding section are correct, then the deep structure of a propositional core sentence such as:

35. The man put the car in the garage.

will effectively look like that given in Figure 5. Rather than use actually occurring variable expressions of English (for example, *someone* or *something*), we have reverted to the use of letters of the alphabet, as in Chapter 3. We may now ask: What information is carried by these variables? The answer is, apparently, that the variables carry information concerning the reference of the expression which ultimately is substituted for them. If, in fact, we examine some of the expressions we wrote in Chapter 3 that made use of variables, we note that we made

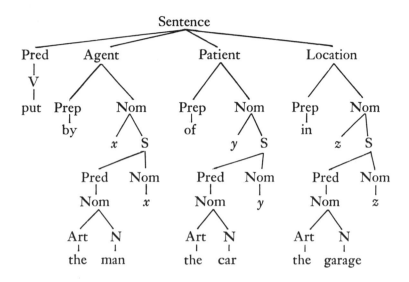

Pred	predicate
V	verb
Prep	preposition
Nom	nominal expression
S	sentence
N	noun
Art	article
Part	particle

Figure 5.   Deep structure of example 35.

use of this very property. Consider, for example, sentence 9 of Chapter 3, repeated here as 36, and the expression based on it that made use of variables, repeated here as 37:

36. Harriet is aware that the boss is fond of her.
37. Aware [x, Fond (y, x)].

In 37, it will be noted, we used x wherever there was an expression in 36 referring to the person named Harriet, and y for the expression referring to the person called the boss. But it is apparent that the pronoun *her* in 36 need not necessarily refer to Harriet (as was assumed when we translated 36 into 37); it could refer to some third person, whom we may designate as z. If that is the case, then 36 is to be translated as:

38. Aware [x, Fond (y, z)].

If the same person or thing is referred to twice within the same simple sentence in English, then generally a reflexive pronoun is used for the second occurrence. Accordingly, the sentence:

39. Harry admires himself.

is translated into:

40. Admires (x, x).

On the other hand, the sentence:

41. Harry admires him.

must be translated into:

42. Admires (x, y).

A problem arises, however, when we attempt to translate the following sentence:

43. Harry admires Harry.

Sentence 43 may be interpreted in two ways. Under what is perhaps the more usual interpretation, the two occurrences of *Harry* are assumed to refer to different individuals, so that the sentences is to be translated into 42. Under the other interpretation, the two occurrences of *Harry* are assumed to refer to the same individual (such an interpretation is more likely if the sentence is said with heavy stress on the second occurrence of *Harry*), in which case 40 is the correct translation.

The fact that the same nominal expression, for example *John*, can be used to refer to two (or arbitrarily many) different entities shows that reference is independent of whatever nominal expression is used. Conversely, the same person or thing can be referred to by many different expressions—the expressions *George Washington*, *General Washington*, *the first president of the United States*, *the man whose picture is on one-dollar bills*, and *Martha Washington's husband* can all be used to refer to the same person. This provides further reason for separating reference from nominal expression in deep structures.

There are, however, certain problems associated with the view that the structure underlying a nonpredicate noun is a variable plus a relative clause containing the corresponding predicate noun—problems that force us to modify this view somewhat. First, notice that there are no expressions in English which make pure reference. (Even the indefinite pronouns *someone* and *something* convey more information than that of reference; in particular, they convey information about whether the referent is a person or a thing.) If it is indeed the case that underlying every nonpredicate nominal expression is a variable plus a relative clause, it is surprising that variables as such never turn up in the surface structures of English sentences. Second, just as in the case of predicate-noun sentences, we need to distinguish between what a sentence containing a nonpredicate noun asserts and what it assumes (compare Chapter 4, Section 2). Consider, for example:

44. My neighbor is handsome.
45. My neighbor isn't handsome.

In 44, it is assumed that my neighbor is a man, and it is asserted that he is good-looking; in 45, the assumption remains that my neighbor is a man, and it is denied that he is good-looking. These facts are not captured if the deep structure of 44 is given as:

46. *x* [*x* is my neighbor] is handsome.

(The brackets in 46 enclose the underlying relative clause—aspects of the deep structure of 44 that are not relevant to the discussion at hand have been omitted.) They are captured, however, if the deep structure is represented as:

47. The man [the man is my neighbor] is handsome.

In other words, the structure underlying a surface nominal expression is an expression consisting of a noun that embodies the assumptions of the main predicate and a relative clause containing the predicate nominal expression that corresponds to the surface nominal expression. Since every predicate makes some assumption about each of the nominal expressions which are associated with it, it follows that English has no need of expressions that, like variables in logic, are used solely for referential purposes.

†5. Some Problems of Reference

Up to now, we have been operating under the assumption that every nominal expression in a sentence makes reference to something. But this is not true. Consider the sentence:

48. Joey wants a pair of skates for Christmas.

Sentence 48 could, by a slight stretch of the imagination, be interpreted to mean that there is a particular pair of skates that Joey wants for Christmas, but the usual interpretation would be that he has no particular skates in mind—anything that would pass for a pair of skates will do. The following rather awkward paraphrase probably conveys what is intended:

49. Joey wants anything such that it is a pair of skates for Christmas.

In other words, the expression *a pair of skates* in 48 is not (under the usual interpretation of that sentence) a referring expression. Another way to appreciate this fact is to consider the following example:

50. Joey wants a unicorn for a pet.

Notice that one could affirm sentence 50 in all honesty without committing oneself to the belief that unicorns exist. Contrast this with:

51. Joey caught a unicorn in the Black Forest.

To affirm 51 is to commit oneself to a belief in the existence of unicorns. The expression that occurs as the direct object of the verb *want* need not be a referring expression, whereas the object of *catch* must be. For further discussion see item 13.

If we take 49 to be a stylistic variant of 48, we observe that the indefinite pronoun, which is used in English to express a nonreferring variable, is a form that makes use of *any* rather than *some* (we postpone further discussion of the *some/any* distinction until Chapter 6). The rules that Bach postulated operate here as well, except that they may have to be generalized so as to be able to delete such expressions as *such that it is* as well as ordinary sequences of relative pronouns and forms of the verb *be*.

Normally, when one substitutes one expression for another where both expressions refer to the same thing, one obtains a sentence which is true only if the original is true. Thus, if it is agreed that *Sarah* and *the boss's daughter* designate the same person, then if I affirm the truth of:

52. John knows that the boss's daughter is ravishing.

I also vouch for the truth of:

53. John knows that Sarah is ravishing.

However, if I affirm:

54. John believes that the boss's daughter is ravishing.

I do not necessarily affirm:

55. John believes that Sarah is ravishing.

The reason for this is simply that if *Sarah* and *the boss's daughter*, are the same person, John cannot *know* that they are different people, whereas he can very well *believe* that they are different people. We say that any nominal expression that occurs in the object clause of the verb *believe* is in a "referentially opaque" position, while any such expression which occurs in the object clause of the verb *know* is in a "referentially transparent" position (these are the terms that are traditionally used by philosophers). As we have presented them so far, neither the later generative-transformational approach, in which nominal expressions are introduced directly, nor the approach proposed by Bach is capable of representing the difference between referentially transparent and referentially opaque contexts. The latter approach is fairly easy to modify, however, so as to make the distinction representable. Referentially opaque contexts basically permit the introduction of the beliefs of different persons: the speaker, the person or persons who play roles in the sentence under consideration, or people in general. Referentially transparent contexts admit only those of the speaker (and also perhaps of people in general). Let us say that nominal expressions such as *the boss's daughter* are transformationally introduced into non-predicate positions not from relative clauses which start out in deep structures as:

56. *x* is (was, etc.) the boss's daughter.

but rather from any of the following:

57. According to me, *x* is (was, etc.) the boss's daughter.
58. According to *y* (where *y* occurs elsewhere in the sentence), *x* is (was, etc.) the boss's daughter.
59. According to people in general, *x* is (was, etc.) the boss's daughter.

Now consider examples 52–55 in the light of this proposed

modification. Let us say it is my belief, as well as that of people in general (but not that of John's), that the boss's daughter and Sarah are the same person (designated by x), whereas it is John's belief that they are different persons (designated by z and w). Since nominal expressions in object clauses of *know* are referentially transparent, only *my* beliefs are tolerated, and since, according to me, the boss's daughter and Sarah are the same person, I am obliged to vouch for the truth of 52 and 53 together. On the other hand, the deep structure underlying 54 (and similarly 55) can be taken to be either:

60. John believes that x, who, according to me, is the boss's daughter, is ravishing.

or:

61. John believes that z, who, according to him, is the boss's daughter, is ravishing.

If by 54, I intend 60, and similarly for 55, then I affirm 54 and 55 together. But if by 54 I intend 61, and similarly for 55, then I do not affirm 54 and 55 together unless it turns out that the persons who John thinks are the boss's daughter and Sarah are, according to him, both ravishing!

The foregoing account does not solve all of the many interesting linguistic and philosophic problems concerning the nature of nonreferring expressions and of referential opacity, but it does indicate an approach that may be fruitful in attempting to reach such solutions. (For further consideration of these matters, see items 14–15.)

†6. Various Uses for Nominal Expressions

An interesting ambiguity arises in certain sentences containing descriptive nominal expressions, for example:

62. John's murderer must have been insane.

63. I will flunk the third person from the end of the second row.

Both of these sentences are ambiguous, depending upon whether the expressions *John's murderer* and *the third person from the end of the second row* are being used to describe an individual already known to the speaker, or are being used as labels for individuals whose identity is not yet known to the speaker. Under the latter interpretation, we can add to 62 and 63 the additional expression *whovever he is*, but not under the former. Indeed, under the latter interpretation 62 and 63 are synonymous with:

64. Whoever was John's murderer must have been insane.
65. I will flunk whoever is the third person from the end of the second row.

whereas under the former interpretation the sentences mean:

66. The one whom I recognize to be John's murderer must have been insane.
67. I will flunk the one whom I recognize to be the third person from the end of the second row.

It is apparent that the ambiguity of 62 and 63 can be accounted for if part (*a*) of Bach's proposal (see Section 3) is extended to allow the deletion of the expression *whoever is* (*was*, etc.).

There is still, however, a difference between *John's murderer* and *the third person from the end of the second row* when these are taken to be labels for persons whose identity is not already known: the latter can be used as a set of instructions for identifying the person who fits the description (if he exists). Expressions for mathematical quantities that cannot be expressed as rational numbers (*the square root of two, the ratio of the circumference to the diameter of a circle*, and the like) can be thought of in a similar way, namely, as representing deep structures (*whatever is the square root of two*) in which the predicate specifies a calculation that, if carried out, would identify the numerical entity in question.

7. Pronouns

Any account of how nominal expressions are used in English must come to grips with the properties of pronouns. The personal pronouns (*I*, *you*, *he*, *she*, *it*, *we*, *they*, and the objective, reflexive, and possessive forms *me*, *myself*, *my*, *mine*, and so on) are used primarily for referential purposes, although they do convey some information about the person, number, and gender of their referent. The traditional view concerning pronouns is that they replace repeated occurrences of nominal expressions within sentences and within longer stretches of speech. This view was taken over by generative-transformational grammarians in the form of a belief that there is a pronominalization transformation, the effect of which is to convert sentences like 68 below into sentences like 69:

68. *The man who was mixing cement* fell into the cement that *the man who was mixing cement* was making.
69. *The man who was mixing cement* fell into the cement that *he* was making.

The expression *the man who was mixing cement* in 69 is called the antecedent of the pronoun *he* in 69. The pronominalization transformation is also assumed to be applicable to sentences like 43—assuming both occurrences of *Harry* in it refer to the same individual—to produce 41. A subsequent reflexivization transformation then applies obligatorily, to produce 39.

The clearest account of English pronominalization from this point of view is to be found in the article by Robert B. Lees and Edward S. Klima entitled "Rules for English Pronominalization." However, more recent research on pronominalization by various generative grammarians, notably Ronald

Langacker and John R. Ross (see item 16) has shown that a number of refinements must be made in Lees and Klima's formulation. For example, Lees and Klima failed to provide for the possibility, illustrated in examples 70–73 below, that a pronoun can, under certain circumstances, precede its antecedent:

70. As soon as *he* got home, *John* ate supper.
71. The fact that *he* has no chance of winning the election does not discourage *the candidate*.
72. Boys who date *them* say that *blondes* are fun.
73. I gave the book that *she* wanted to *Mary*.

In each of these examples, the italicized expressions are intended to refer to the same entity or entities. If one examines these sentences carefully, one discovers that in all of them, the pronoun occurs in a subordinate clause that does not include the antecedent, whereas the antecedent is not in a clause that includes the pronoun. On the other hand, if one examines certain sentences in which these conditions are not met, one discovers that a pronoun cannot be used to refer to a following antecedent:

74. *He said that *the candidate* was optimistic.
75. *I gave *her* the book that *Mary* wanted.

On the basis of these and similar examples, it is tempting to conclude, as did Ross and Langacker, that a pronoun can refer to a following antecedent just in case it is included in a subordinate clause which does not include the antecedent. However, as George Lakoff, Paul Postal, and others have pointed out in recent work, there are a considerable number of cases in which a pronoun can refer to a following antecedent even though it is not in a clause subordinate to the one which contains the antecedent. Consider, for example:

76. *His* portrait doesn't do *the old man* justice.
77. It was *his* accent that betrayed *Gustav*.
78. Near *him*, *John* discovered a wasp's nest.

79. John still refuses to speak to *her*, although *Mary* has admitted that she was at fault.

Examples 76–79 show that a pronoun can indeed refer to a following antecedent even though it is not contained in a subordinate clause not including the antecedent. Upon reviewing examples like 76–79, and certain others, Lakoff has recently concluded that the relationship between pronouns and antecedents is not governed by transformational rules at all, but by general conditions, called output conditions, that govern the general form of surface structures. A consequence of this view is that pronouns, rather than being introduced transformationally, are introduced directly as such within deep structures.

†8. Additional Arguments that Pronouns Are Introduced Directly

The view that pronouns are introduced directly in deep structures is supported by other considerations as well. First, pronouns that simply have no antecedents must be introduced in deep structures in any event. There is no rule of English grammar that prevents anyone from starting his conversation with the remark:

80. He looks like a movie star.

Second, we can construct sentences in which we get into an infinite regress if we attempt to replace the pronouns by the antecedents they are supposed to be the transforms of. Such sentences are called Bach-Peters sentences, after their "discoverers," Emmon Bach and Stanley Peters. The following is a typical Bach-Peters sentence:

81. The man who was mixing it fell into the cement he was making.

in which the antecedent of *it* is taken to be *the cement he was making*, and the antecedent of *he* is taken to be *the man who was mixing it.* Since each pronoun is contained in the antecedent of the other, when the antecedent of one of them is substituted, the other is introduced, so that it is impossible to eliminate the pronouns by substituting their antecedents back in for them! Thus, upon substituting the antecedent of *it* in the expression *the man who was mixing it*, we obtain *the man who was mixing the cement he was making*; substituting the antecedent of *he* in that expression, we obtain *the man who was mixing the cement the man who was mixing it was making.* Clearly there is no end to this process. We conclude that we cannot consider pronouns to be substitutes for expressions that are identical to their antecedents, since if we did, it would be impossible to state the deep structures of Bach-Peters sentences.

Like other nominal expressions, then, pronouns originate in deep structures either as predicates in relative clauses (when they are used to assert particular information about their referents), or directly as embodiments of the assumptions of the sentences as a whole. They are probably used more commonly in the latter function; indeed the distinctions that are made in the English personal pronominal system (animate or human vs. inanimate; male vs. female; singular vs. plural) are precisely those which are most characteristic of assumptions. (See also items 17–20.)

9. Collective and Plural Nouns and the Concept of Deep Structure Groups

In our discussion up to the present, nominal expressions have been used that, by and large, make reference to individual entities. But of course such expressions can be used in English to make reference to more than one entity, or to an entity that designates a group of individuals, as in the following sentences:

82. *Alan, Bob, and Charlie* were waiting for a bus.
83. *Three men* were waiting for a bus.
84. *A small group* was waiting for a bus.

Moreover, there are predicates that assume a group designation for entities that play particular roles in connection with them. Consider, for example, the following sentences:

85. *The mob* assembled in the square.
86. Christ distributed the loaves *to his disciples.*
87. *Jack and Irene* are an interesting pair.
88. *My friends* are numerous.
89. *The train and the bus* collided.

In 85–89, the italicized expressions designate entities that are assumed to be groups of individual entities by virtue of the main predicate used with each of them. The verb *assemble* requires that the expression which designates its patient be a group of individual entities; similarly, *distribute* requires that its goal be a group (notice also that example 86 asserts that each disciple received at least one loaf, or at least part of a loaf). The predicate *pair* assumes of its essive subject at least that it designates a group; it may also be interpreted to assume that it designates exactly two people (asserting only that the two go together in some way). *Numerous*, on the other hand, assumes that its subject designates a group of indefinite number, and asserts that that number is large. The following sentences are therefore odd because they violate the assumption regarding indefiniteness of number:

90. Alan, Bob, Charlie, Dick, and Edward are numerous.
91. The five men are numerous.
92. The quintet is numerous.

Finally, *collide* requires that its patient designate a group, as we pointed out in Chapter 4.

In Chapter 4, too, we proposed a notation for representing the role structures of predicates that require one or more of their roles to be expressed by groups; such roles are to be enclosed in angle brackets. Using this notation, we state below the role structures of *assemble* and *distribute*:

93. *assemble*: ⟨Patient⟩, Location, (Agent)
94. *distribute*: Patient, ⟨Goal⟩, Agent

In order to state the role structure of *pair*, we need, in addition, a way of indicating that its essive subject designates exactly two entities; we do this by subscripting the numeral 2 to the angle brackets enclosing the role in the statement of its role structure, as follows:

95. *pair*: ⟨Essive⟩$_2$

In general, we use a subscript on angle brackets to indicate the number of entities in a group, and the absence of a subscript can be interpreted to mean that the number may be indefinite. If a predicate, such as *numerous*, requires that one of its roles have an indefinite number, that fact can be indicated by a subscripted *i*:

96. *numerous*: ⟨Patient⟩$_i$

From the examples that have been given, it will be observed that the nominal expressions used to designate groups include those based on collective nouns, such as *mob*; plural nouns, such as *disciples*; and conjunctions, such as *Jack and Irene*. Expressions introduced by quantifying words, such as *all of the men, none of the men, both men*, are also so used, but in a somewhat different way. Although the expression *both men* is used to designate a group of two men, it is odd to say:

97. Both men are an interesting pair.

The reason is that one uses the expression *both men* only when referring to the properties of each man in the group, and being *an interesting pair* is not a property that an individual can have. There are many interesting and some as yet unsolved problems concerning the grammar of expressions that designate groups; a couple of these are raised in items 21–23.

10. Definite, Indefinite, and Generic Expressions

We conclude this chapter by briefly considering the characteristics of nominal expressions having to do with the choice of article (*the* vs. *a* or *an*). Let us begin by considering predicate nominal expressions.
If we compare the sentences:

98. Vince is an heir to Max's fortune.
99. Vince is the heir to Max's fortune.

we notice right away that one of the assumptions of sentence 99 with the definite article is that there is exactly one heir to Max's fortune, whereas one of the assumptions of sentence 98 with the indefinite article is that there is at least one heir to the fortune. Similarly, in:

100. The Mazetti brothers are heirs to Max's fortune.
101. The Mazetti brothers are the heirs to Max's fortune.

we observe that when the subject designates a group, the definite article is used when it is assumed that there is exactly one group of heirs to Max's fortune, and the indefinite article (which is not realized phonetically) when there is at least one group. When it is common knowledge that a particular predicate, for example *capital of the United States*, designates a unique entity at a particular point in time, then the definite article is almost invariably used with it:

102. Washington, D.C. is the capital of the United States.

The proviso "at a particular point in time" is necessary, since there have been other United States capitals in the past. Similarly, the use of the definite article when the noun is modified by a superlative adjective is accounted for, since a superlative is used only when it is assumed that the total nominal expression designates a unique entity or class of entities:

103. The sit-in at the administration building was the most significant event of the week on campus.

Indeed, the use of contrastively stressed *the* has come to take on a superlative sense, as in the sentence:

104. The sit-in at the administration building was *the* event of the week on campus.

When objects of predicate nouns are converted into prenominal genitive expressions, the genitive expression replaces the definite article. To see this, consider example 106 from Chapter 3, repeated here as example 105:

105. Princess Grace is Prince Rainier's wife.

It is clear that one of the assumptions of 105 is that Prince Rainier has exactly one wife, so that 105 is a stylistic variant of 106 but not of 107:

106. Princess Grace is the wife of Prince Rainier.
107. Princess Grace is a wife of Prince Rainier.

It is important to realize that even if the predicate nominal expression is definite, the subject does not have to be. Consider, for example:

108. A friend of mine is the heir to Max's fortune.

Sentence 108, like 99, assumes that there is exactly one heir to Max's fortune; it asserts that the individual is one of a group comprising friends of mine. The sentence also assumes that I have at least one friend—this follows from the use of the indefinite article in a nonpredicate nominal expression, that is, the subject of 108.

Conversely, a definite expression can be used as subject of an indefinite predicate; sentence 100 is an example of such usage. So, for that matter, is 98, since a proper name is generally (note: not always) used with the assumption that it designates exactly one individual or one group of individuals.

If we now examine nonpredicate nominal expressions, we find that the definite and indefinite articles are used in them under the same conditions as in predicate nominal expressions:

109. Brutus killed a tyrant.
110. Brutus killed the tyrant.
111. A man who was standing by the door just collapsed.
112. The man who was standing by the door just collapsed.

The assumptions of 110 and 112 are, respectively, that for purposes of the discussions in which they may be used, *tyrant* designates exactly one individual and *man who was standing by the door* designates exactly one individual. For effective communication to take place, a speaker of either of these sentences must assume that his hearer can identify the intended referent. In 109 and 111, on the other hand, it is assumed that there is a class consisting of at least one individual such that *tyrant* or *man who was standing by the door* can be used to designate any of them.

The assumptions that particular predicates make about the entities which fulfill their roles are always of an indefinite sort. For example, the adjective *handsome* assumes that its subject designates *a* male being, not *the* male being. There are, in fact, no predicates that assume the definiteness (that is, uniqueness) of the entities which bear a semantic relationship to them.

There are contexts in which it is possible to use definite singular, indefinite singular, and indefinite plural nominal expressions interchangeably. Consider the following examples:

113. The elephant never forgets.
114. An elephant never forgets.
115. Elephants never forget.

Examples 113–115 all have an interpretation that can be expressed thus:

116. If something is an elephant it never forgets.

When interpreted as 116, we say that sentences 113–115 belong to the class of generic sentences, and that the nominal expressions in them are also generic. Rather than conveying different assumptions, the definite and indefinite articles in this type of generic expression differ only stylistically. For consideration of the transformational apparatus needed to account for generic sentences, see Chapter 6, Section 2.

11. Concluding Remarks

In this chapter, we have gone to some lengths to deal with the enormously difficult problem of how to account syntactically for the properties of nominal expressions in sentences. This has been done primarily because it has not been generally realized that there is any particular difficulty in this area of grammar. Furthermore, the topics which have been touched on here are now at the frontier of linguistic research, particularly the problems relating to assumption and assertion; reference; the use of pronouns, sets and individuals; and the use of the articles.

The next chapter deals exclusively with what a transformational rule is, what transformations are intended to account for, and how they relate to the other rules of grammar—those having to do with the construction of sentences out of predicates and role structures. It is designed to tie up some of the loose ends of Chapter 4 and of this chapter, and to take us out of the realm of propositional core sentences, within which we have been largely confined so far (although not so much in this chapter).

PROBLEMS AND SUGGESTIONS FOR FURTHER STUDY

1. The case for the transformational introduction of non-predicate nominal expressions has been made by Emmon Bach in his article "Nouns and Noun Phrases," in Bach and Harms (eds.), *Universals in Linguistic Theory*. Also see James McCawley, "Where Do Noun Phrases Come From?" in Roderick Jacobs and Peter Rosenbaum (eds.), *Readings in English Transformational Grammar*; Paul Postal, "Problems in the Linguistic Representation of Reference," in Danny Steinberg and Leon Jakobovits (eds.), *Semantics*, forthcoming.

2. Given that examples 3 and 4 of this chapter are ambiguous, do you think examples 1 and 2 are? If not, why not?

3. Identify the role played by *this statue* in the sentence:

    117. This statue is marble.

4. In general, the role structures of nouns derived from verbs are related to the role structures of those verbs

(see the discussion of examples 15–17). Using the following examples, develop the role structures of the verb *invent* and the related nouns *inventor* and *invention*.

118. Edison invented the incandescent bulb.
119. Edison was the inventor of the incandescent bulb.
120. The incandescent bulb was Edison's invention.
121. One of the most important developments in American technology was Edison's invention of the incandescent bulb.

5. In a sentence such as:

122. This is a carton of eggs.

it is not clear whether what is being pointed out is a carton or eggs. Also, when a sentence like 122 is used as a source for the nonpredicate expression *a carton of eggs*, the potential ambiguity may be retained. Consider, for example, the following sentences:

123. I opened a carton of eggs.
124. I scrambled a carton of eggs.
125. I broke a carton of eggs.

Show that these facts can be explained if it is assumed that either *carton* or *eggs* can be substituted for the underlying variable in 123–125. We say that the noun substituted for the variable is the "head" of the nominal expression.

6. Use your solution to problem 5 to account for the ambiguity of the sentence:

126. I inspected fifty cartons of eggs.

7. Can clauses be used as predicates? Consider such examples as:

127. The truth is that neither candidate can win.
128. John's idea is to call for a general strike.

8. It is clear from considering sentences such as:

> 129. That isn't an alligator.

that different aspects of the meaning of *alligator*, and for that matter of any noun, can be assumed depending upon the context. Thus, when 129 is uttered by a zoologist under the proper circumstances, it is assumed that the thing is a reptile and denies that it has the characteristics that, say, distinguish an alligator from a crocodile. On the other hand, when uttered by a little boy in a boat in the Everglades, it is assumed only that the thing is a physical object. Is it therefore necessary to clutter up our dictionaries with long sets of alternatives (like 21), or can you develop a rule that operates on a single definition and informs us what the set of different assumptions may be with respect to that definition?

9. Give a technical and a nontechnical definition of *fraction*.

10. Give other examples that work like 27–29; 27 is repeated here for convenience:

> 27. John's wife was born at home.

What form of the verb *be* do you think has been deleted in the following sentence (commonly used among baseball announcers):

> 130. The tying run is on third base.

†11. What paradox would arise if variables could be predicates? As the following examples show, it is indeed possible to use the indefinite pronouns *someone* and *something* as predicates, but then do they have the same meaning (that is, are they the same lexical items) as the nonpredicate indefinite pronouns?

> 131. Mary's party was something.
> 132. My father is someone in this town.

12. How are the relationships between the following pairs of sentences best accounted for:

    133. Princess Grace was formerly Grace Kelly.
    134. Princess Grace is the former Grace Kelly.
    135. These ladies have been my friends for some time.
    136. These ladies are my old friends.
    137. She will be Miss America sometime.
    138. She is a future Miss America.
    139. Mary was once a girlfriend of John's.
    140. Mary is an ex-girlfriend of John's.

Notice that the adjectives *former*, *old*, and *future* in 134, 136, and 138 cannot be used predicatively as such.

13. What role is being played by objects of verbs such as *want*, where the speaker is not necessarily committed to the existence of the entities usually referred to by those objects? What preposition is usually associated with this role? Hint—compare such sentences as:

    141. Harold is listening to a signal.
    142. Harold is listening for a signal.

†14. Explain why it is that when someone says:

    143. Monroe knows that Paris is the capital of Sweden.

he is betraying his own ignorance as well as Monroe's, whereas when he says:

    144. Monroe thinks that Paris is the capital of Sweden.

only Monroe's ignorance is revealed.

†15. Using the theory of referential opacity developed in the text, account for the difference between the following two sentences, and for the fact that both are grammatical (the examples are due to James McCawley):

    145. I dreamed that I was Brigitte Bardot and that I kissed me.

146. I dreamed that I was Brigitte Bardot and that I kissed myself.

16. For recent important discussion of problems relating to pronominalization, see Ronald Langacker, "Pronominalization and the Chain of Command," and J. R. Ross, "On the Cyclic Nature of English Pronominalization," both in D. Reibel and S. Schane (eds.), *Modern Studies in English.* Also see my *Study of Syntax*, Chapter 5.

17. What is the difference in meaning between:

147. Judy lost a dollar bill and I found it.
148. Judy lost a dollar bill and I found one.

On the relationship between the indefinite article *a* (*an*) and *one*, see David Perlmutter, "On the Article in English," in M. Bierwisch and K. Heidolph (eds.), *Recent Advances in Linguistics.*

†18. Show that it is difficult, if not impossible, to construct Bach-Peters sentences if the two pronouns are the same (for example, both are *them, it, him*).

19. Consider the sentence:

149. Since John couldn't get hold of Bill by telephone, he went to see him.

If 149 is spoken with normal intonation, and no gestures are made by the speaker, the antecedent of *he* is taken to be *John*, and the antecedent of *him* is taken to be *Bill*. Suppose that you wanted to say instead:

150. Since John couldn't get hold of Bill by telephone, Bill went to see John.

and that you wanted to use pronouns in the main clause. How would you have to say it?

†20. If we take the position that the assumptions predicates make about the entities that play roles in connection

with them are embodied as nominal expressions introduced directly as such in deep structures, why are we then obliged to recognize the existence of a pronominalization transformation after all? Consider, for example, such a sentence as:

151. They got married.

Is the Bach-Peters paradox avoided?

21. For a clear, philosophically oriented treatment of quantified nominal expressions, see Zeno Vendler, "Each and Every, Any and All," in his *Linguistics and Philosophy*.

22. We noticed in Chapter 2 that people tend to use plural pronouns when their antecedents are quantified expressions such as *everyone* and *no one*. How can the tendency be accounted for?

23. What is the difference in meaning between the sentences:

152. In our family, everyone loves everyone.
153. In our family, everyone loves himself.

How is this difference to be represented in deep structure?

24. A few proper names (for example, *The Bronx*, *The Hague*, *The Narrows*) have the definite article incorporated into them. Why aren't there proper names incorporating the indefinite article?

25. There are constructions in which only indefinite nominal expressions are used. Consider, for example:

154. There is an abundance of talent in the present administration.
155. John has a tooth missing.

It would be odd to put *the* for *a* or *an* in the foregoing examples. Can you think of an explanation?

6

SYNTACTIC TRANSFOR- MATIONS

According to the theoretical point of view that has been developed in Chapters 4 and 5, English syntax consists of those rules which convert the abstract semantic, or semantically interpreted, structure of sentences into their manifest, or physical, form. These rules are transformational, in the sense given to that term in Chapter 3, so that we shall find ourselves referring to the rules not only as rules of syntax but also as transformational rules, or, more simply, as transformations. Among other things, transformations account for: the different forms that sentences both inside and outside the propositional core of English take on (initially discussed in Chapter 3); the introduction of nominal expressions into sentences (discussed in Chapter 5); the placement of the nominal expressions that fill the various roles of the predicate verb, noun, or adjective in sentences (discussed in Chapter 4). In this chapter, we shall look carefully at a variety of transformational rules that perform these and various other functions, in order to determine how they operate and, more important, why they operate as they do. A great deal is known about both these matters, but much, much more is not. We begin by considering a few relatively well-understood syntactic phenomena, for which a relatively straightforward transformational account can be given.

1. Examples of Transformations

Let us consider first the phenomena discussed in Chapter 3 in connection with examples 7 and 55 and in items 13 and 14. It was noted that a transformation in English, called the particle-movement transformation, relates such sentences as:

1. The doctor took off the patient's bandages.
2. The doctor took the patient's bandages off.

Sentences 1 and 2 have the same meaning and contain the same lexical items. It may therefore be assumed that they share a common deep structure, and that the operation of the particle-movement transformation in one, but not the other, of these sentences accounts for the difference in their manifest syntactic form. Moreover, it seems reasonable to assume that the rule has applied to example 2, rather than to 1, since it seems intuitively clear that the elements *took* and *off* function together semantically as a unit, with the meaning, roughly, of a single-word verb *removed*. In example 1 these elements appear adjacent to one another, but not in 2; therefore we conclude that in 2, the particle *off* has been moved to the end of the sentence by the particle-movement transformation. Our task now, as English grammarians, is to determine as precisely as possible how this rule operates, and to raise the question why it operates the way it does.

If we consider just examples 1 and 2, and others like them, we would conclude that the particle-movement transformation operates to move a particle associated with the main verb of a sentence to a position immediately following the direct object. If we let the symbol *V* stand for any verb, *Part* for any particle, and *Nom* for any nominal expression, we may state the transformation symbolically as follows:

3.
$$\begin{array}{ccc} V & Part & Nom \\ 1 & 2 & 3 \end{array} \longrightarrow \quad 1 \quad \emptyset \quad 3 + 2$$

The numbers *1*, *2*, and *3* in the statement of this rule refer to the elements that take part in the operation of the rule; the rule itself states that the second constituent (the particle) is deleted in its original position and is added to the sentence immediately following the third constituent (the nominal expression functioning as direct object). Since the failure to apply the rule does not lead to ungrammaticality (note that example 1, to which the rule has not applied, is grammatical), we conclude that the rule is optional, in the sense given to that term in Chapter 3, Section 4.

To arrive at a precise statement of the rule, however—one that is accurate for the English language as a whole—we need to examine other sorts of sentences than those which are exactly like 1 and 2. Suppose the direct object is the pronoun *them* rather than the full nominal expression *the patient's bandages*. We notice that the rule is apparently obligatory, since the failure to apply the particle-movement transformation results in sentences like 4, which are, in standard English at least, ungrammatical:

4.*The doctor took off them.

On the other hand, suppose the direct object is a complex nominal expression containing a relative clause, for example *the bandages which had become encrusted with blood*. We observe that, in general, three different sentences are possible: one in which the particle is not moved at all, one in which the particle is moved after the entire nominal expression, and one in which the particle is moved to a position between the head noun of the nominal expression and the relative clause. Thus:

5. The doctor took off the bandages which had become encrusted with blood.

6. The doctor took the bandages which had become encrusted with blood off.
7. The doctor took the bandages off which had become encrusted with blood.

Of these sentences, example 6, in which the particle appears to have been moved beyond the entire nominal expression, seems somewhat unnatural and clumsy, whereas the other two seem perfectly natural and grammatical. This state of affairs becomes clearer as soon as we consider examples in which the relative clause itself ends in a particle:

8. The doctor took off the bandages which someone else had previously put on.
9. ?The doctor took the bandages which someone else had previously put on off.
10. The doctor took the bandages off which someone else had previously put on.

Here there can be no dispute that the movement of the particle to a position following the entire complex nominal expression results in an extremely awkward, and perhaps even ungrammatical, sentence.

We are faced, then, with the following problem: The particle-movement transformation as initially set up in 3 yields sentences, such as 6 and 9, whose grammatical status is questionable; it also fails to account for other sentences, such as 7 and 10, in which the particle ends up between the two parts of the direct-object nominal expression. Two ways to solve this problem immediately suggest themselves. First, we could revise the statement of the particle-movement transformation so that it would directly put the particle between the head noun and relative clause of a complex direct-object nominal expression. Second, we could let the particle-movement transformation stand as it is in 3, and set up a second transformation to move relative clauses around particles. According to this solution, the particle-movement transformation applies to the structure corresponding to sentences like 5 and

8 to produce 6 and 9, and this new transformation, call it the relative-clause-movement transformation, applies to 6 and 9 to produce 7 and 10. Is there any evidence which would lead us to prefer one of these solutions to the other?

It turns out that there is evidence to indicate quite clearly that the second of these solutions is to be preferred. Consider the following pair of sentences:

11. The man who was supposed to introduce the speaker hasn't arrived yet.
12. The man hasn't arrived yet who was supposed to introduce the speaker.

Examples 11 and 12 are synonymous—they have the same deep structure and their surface structures differ only in that the relative clause, which is part of the subject nominal expression, has been moved in 12 to the end of the sentence. To account for these facts, we must set up some sort of transformation to move the relative clause in 12 from its original position as part of the subject of the sentence to a position at the end of the sentence. Without going into details, we can see that the transformation required for this purpose is precisely the same rule required under the second solution to the problem just discussed concerning particle movement, namely, the relative-clause-movement transformation. But this means that the second solution to the problem concerning particle movement is to be preferred, since it (a) makes use of a rule needed in English grammar on independent grounds, and (b) does not force us to complicate in any way the statement of the particle-movement transformation.

The foregoing argument is characteristic of much of the reasoning that goes into the establishment of rules of syntax by contemporary grammarians. A tentative statement of some rule needed to account for a certain range of facts is set up. A wider range of facts is then examined, and it is noticed that the rule may be incapable of handling those facts. The grammarian then examines the options that are open to him: restating the original rule in a somewhat more complicated way, or finding evidence that the new facts are the result of the interaction of his original rule with some other rule or rules of grammar. The outcome of his investigation may be that the original rule is left intact (as in the case just discussed), or it may be that the original rule is changed in some way. For further consideration of these matters, see problems 3–6.

Why a particular transformation operates in the way that it does turns out to be a much more difficult and subtle question than how it operates. For one thing, it does very little good to look at a single rule of grammar and ask the question why; one can only begin to find satisfactory answers by examining rules in the light of the grammar as a whole. The answers also depend upon knowing answers to questions which, properly speaking, lie outside the domain of linguistics. For example, we need to know whether it is easier to perceive and comprehend sentences when their constituents are arranged in a particular way rather than in some other way. If so, then perhaps that is one reason why a particular transformation applies in a certain way. Although we now have some knowledge about such matters as the perception and comprehension of sentences, we are still a long way from having a sufficient basis on which to build an explanatory theory of syntax.

Let us now consider a transformational rule of English for which a partial explanation of the nature of its operation can be given. This transformation deletes the relative pronoun or particle that introduces relative clauses—we call it the relative-pronoun/particle-deletion transformation. Compare the following sentences:

13. The suit which I bought was on sale.
14. The suit that I bought was on sale.
15. The suit I bought was on sale.

In example 13, the relative clause *which I bought*, which modifies the subject noun *suit*, is introduced by the relative pronoun *which*, which stands for the object of the verb *bought* of the relative clause. In 14, the relative clause is introduced instead by the element *that*, which according to some grammarians is to be treated as a relative pronoun exactly like the *which* of 13, and according to others is to be considered merely a clause-introducing particle unrelated to the relative pronoun. The exact status of the word *that* need not concern us here (for some discussion, see Otto Jespersen, *Modern English Grammar*, Vol. 3, pp. 80ff., 153ff). The important point for our purposes here is that example 15, in which the relative clause is neither introduced by a relative pronoun nor by a relative particle, is synonymous with the other two examples. Let us say, then, that there is a transformation in English that optionally deletes the introductory pronoun or particle of relative clauses.

Now let us consider sentences in which the relative pronoun stands for the subject of the relative clause:

16. The only suit which fit me was too expensive.
17. The only suit that fit me was too expensive.

In such cases, the relative-pronoun/particle-deletion transformation is inapplicable; that is, the sentences that would result from its application are ungrammatical:

18.*The only suit fit me was too expensive.

There is, however, a ready explanation for the inapplicability of the transformation in question to the structures represented by examples 16 and 17. Whenever we listen to sentences in speech, we apply a perceptual strategy according to which we automatically interpret a sentence that begins with a nominal expression and a finite verb in such a way that we consider them to be the main subject and the verb of the sentence. If we were to hear example 18 spoken to us, we would interpret the expression *the only suit* as the main subject and the verb *fit* as the main verb of the sentence, contrary to the intention of the speaker, who intended *was* as the main verb of the sentence. This explains why the relative-pronoun/particle-deletion transformation is restricted in its application the way it is; it is inapplicable in just those cases in which it would create sentences whose structures would be misleading to listeners.

Other examples can be given of the effect of the perceptual strategy on the form of English syntax. If we examine clauses that can function directly as subjects or objects of verbs (what Jespersen called "content clauses"), we notice that there are restrictions on the possible deletion of the element *that*, which ordinarily introduces such clauses. When such clauses function as direct objects, the element is freely deletable; consider the following sentences:

19. I think that Uncle Mort must have been out of his mind when he volunteered to mediate that dispute.
20. I think Uncle Mort must have been out of his mind when he volunteered to mediate that dispute.

When, however, they function as subjects, and remain in subject position (that is, before the main verb), the element *that* cannot be deleted:

21. That he will forfeit his bond seems quite certain.
22.*He will forfeit his bond seems quite certain.
23. It seems quite certain that he will forfeit his bond.
24. It seems quite certain he will forfeit his bond.

In example 21, the clause *that he will forfeit his bond* functions as subject of the verb *seems*, and we note that the clause-introductory particle *that* cannot be deleted. In 23, the subject clause has been moved to the end of the sentence as a whole, leaving behind the pronoun *it* in subject position—this is due to the application of a transformation, to be discussed in some detail later on in this chapter, called (again following Jespersen's terminology) the extraposition transformation. Under these conditions, however, the particle *that* is deletable, since example 24, unlike 22, is grammatical.

The explanation for this rather curious restriction on the deletability of the introductory *that* of content clauses is once again based on the perceptual strategy outlined above. If the transformation is permitted to delete the introductory *that* of content clauses in subject positions, then the subject and verb of the content clause will be mistaken by listeners for the main subject and verb of the sentence. In other words, the retention of the *that* in examples like 21 is necessary to insure that the subject content clause will be understood as subordinate to the main clause of which it is part. (For further consideration of the problem of explanation in syntax, see items 7, 8, and 10 at the end of this chapter.)

After this introduction to the subject of syntactic transformations, we proceed to some of the transformational rules that are relevant to the problem of the introduction of nominal expressions into sentences.

2. The Introduction of Nominal Expressions: Relative-Clause Formation

Rather than tackle head-on the problem of how nominal expressions are introduced into sentences, we shall break it up into its components. We ask first how relative clauses are introduced, assuming for the moment that we have already accounted for the introduction of that part of the nominal expression that they modify.

Many grammarians have noted that a sentence containing a noun modified by a relative clause may be paraphrased by a discourse consisting of two sentences, the first corresponding to the relative clause and the second to the main clause. Thus, the sentence:

25. The girl whom my cousin married became pregnant.

corresponds to the discourse:

26. My cousin married a girl. She became pregnant.

On the other hand, the sentence:

27. My cousin married a girl who became pregnant.

corresponds to the discourse:

28. A girl became pregnant. My cousin married her.

In examples 26 and 28, the temporal order of the sentences suggests a corresponding temporal order to the events described in them. Example 26 describes a situation in which a girl becomes pregnant after marriage, and 28 a situation in which she becomes pregnant before marriage. This semantic difference between the discourses carries over into the sentences with relative clauses. Thus, the meaning of 25 differs from that of 27 in precisely the same way that 26 differs from 28. These observations suggest that there is a syntactic, that is, transformational, relationship between 25 and 26 and between 27 and 28. Informally, we can describe that relationship as follows. Take the two-sentence discourses 26 and 28 as basic (closer to deep structure). Given that in each of the two sentences there is a nominal expression that has the same reference, put the first sentence in as a subordinate clause modifying the designated nominal expression in the second. Next, replace the lexical content of the modified expression by the lexical content of the designated expression in the subordinate clause, and replace the latter expression by the appropriate personal pronoun. Next, put the appropriate relative pronoun at the beginning of the subordinate clause. Finally, delete the designated nominal expression in the relative clause. Call this entire operation the relative-clause-formation transformation.

Since the application of this transformation is a relatively complicated matter, let us show how it operates step-by-step in the derivation of example 25 from 26:

29a. (26.) My cousin married a girl. She became pregnant.
29b. She (my cousin married a girl) became pregnant.
29c. The girl (my cousin married her) became pregnant.
29d. The girl (whom my cousin married her) became pregnant.
29e. (25.) The girl (whom my cousin married) became pregnant.

In the discourses 26 and 28, the order of the sentences reflected a difference in the temporal order of events. There are other discourses, however, in which the order of the sentences reflects no such difference and, as would be expected, the sentences formed by the relative-clause-formation transformation also fail to reflect a difference. Consider the discourses:

30. I witnessed an artillery bombardment. It was intense.
31. The artillery bombardment was intense. I witnessed it.

No semantic difference exists between these discourses such as exists between 26 and 28. Similarly, the sentences formed from 30 and 31 by the relative-clause-formation transformation show no difference (that is, they are synonymous):

32. The artillery bombardment that I witnessed was intense.
33. I witnessed an artillery bombardment that was intense.

The foregoing account of the formation of relative clauses actually only deals with one sort of relative clause, those generally called restrictive relative clauses. A restrictive relative clause restricts the potential reference of the modified noun. Thus, the noun *girl* can refer to any relatively young human female, but the phrase *the girl whom my cousin married* refers only to a particular one of these; therefore, the clause *whom my cousin married* is called restrictive. Besides restrictive relative clauses, however, there are also nonrestrictive ones, clauses which do not appear to restrict the potential reference of the modified noun. Consider, for example, the following sentence:

34. Business discriminates against the girl, who is always given a lower salary for the same amount of responsibility.

In example 34, the clause *who is always given a lower salary for the same amount of responsibility* is intended to be taken as true of any girl. A clearer indication of the contrast between restrictive and nonrestrictive relative clauses is provided by the following two examples; in the first, the italicized relative clause is restrictive, and in the second, nonrestrictive:

35. My typewriter *which is in the study* doesn't have a carriage return.

36. My typewriter, *which is in the study*, doesn't have a carriage return.

In 35, it may be assumed that the speaker has more than one typewriter, but that the one being talked about is in the study, whereas in 36 it is assumed that the speaker has exactly one typewriter, and it is furthermore claimed that it is in the study. When we attempt to paraphrase examples 35 and 36 as two sentences, we observe that the difference between restrictive and nonrestrictive relative clauses corresponds, among other things, to a difference in the order of the sentences in the underlying discourse. Thus, 35 corresponds, as do the previous examples, to a discourse in which a sentence corresponding to the relative clause is put first, and a sentence corresponding to the main clause is put second:

37. A typewriter of mine is in the study. It doesn't have a carriage return.

Example 36, on the other hand, corresponds to a discourse in which the relative clause is put second, in the form of an afterthought:

38. My typewriter doesn't have a carriage return. It is in the study.

The crucial difference in the form of the deep structures underlying 35 and 36, however, is that in the restrictive case, the underlying expression used to refer to the speaker's typewriter is indefinite (*a typewriter of mine*), whereas in the nonrestrictive case, it is already definite (*my typewriter*).

But, we still have not provided an adequate syntactic account for the full range of relative-clause types in English. One more type will be dealt with here (for some others, see items 11–13). Consider the sentence:

39. A person who smokes stands a good chance of developing lung cancer.

Quite obviously, example 39 is not a stylistic variant of the discourse 40:

40. A person smokes. He stands a good chance of developing lung cancer.

Rather, it is a variant of the conditional sentence:

41. If a person smokes, he stands a good chance of developing lung cancer.

If we take the conditional form exemplified by 41 as closer to the deep structure than the relative clause form 39, then we require a transformational rule to convert structures like those illustrated by 41 into those illustrated by 39. Such a rule is quite difficult to state formally, or symbolically, but its existence is clearly motivated by the facts. (For further discussion, see items 14–15.)

3. Transformational Reduction of Relative Clauses

In the first section of this chapter ("Examples of Transformations"), we argued that there is a transformational rule in English that may, under certain conditions, delete the relative pronoun or particle. There is also a transformation that deletes a relative pronoun or particle together with any form of the verb *be*—the need for postulating this transformation was discussed in Chapter 5, Section 3. Since, as John R. Ross has observed, relative pronouns generally begin with the letters *wh*, and since *is* (pronounced as if it were spelled *iz*) is a common form of the verb *be*, we may refer to this rule conveniently as "whiz" deletion. According to this rule, then, the following sentences are stylistic variants:

42. The man who is entering the room right now is a spy.
43. The man entering the room right now is a spy.

If, upon application of whiz deletion, all that is left of the original relative clause is an adjective, or an adjective preceded by its modifiers, then the adjective, together with its modifiers, is moved in front of the noun modified. We call the rule that accomplishes this the adjective-preposing transformation. Applying whiz deletion to the structure underlying:

44. John just met a girl who is extremely ravishing.

we obtain:

45.*John just met a girl extremely ravishing.

Then, applying the adjective-preposing transformation, we obtain, finally:

46. John just met an extremely ravishing girl.

The adjective-preposing transformation is inapplicable, however, if the adjective is followed by any constituent, or if the adjective modifies an indefinite pronoun (such as *someone*, *anyone*) rather than a noun. Thus, the application of whiz deletion to:

47. John just met someone who was extremely ravishing.

results in the grammatical sentence:

48. John just met someone extremely ravishing.

The further application of adjective preposing to 48 would result in an ungrammatical sentence:

49.*John just met extremely ravishing someone.

Similarly, the application of whiz deletion to:

50. John just met a girl who was enthusiastic about Sinatra.

results in the grammatical sentence:

51. John just met a girl enthusiastic about Sinatra.

The further application of adjective preposing, whether it affects just the word *enthusiastic* or the entire phrase *enthusiastic about Sinatra*, would result in ungrammaticality:

52.*John just met an enthusiastic girl about Sinatra.

53.*John just met an enthusiastic about Sinatra girl.

It might be objected that we are mistaken to relate transformationally what traditionally have been called attributive adjectives (adjectives that modify nouns) to what have been called predicate adjectives (adjectives that follow the verb *be*) in relative clauses. For one thing, sentences with attributive adjectives are much more "direct" than sentences with predicate adjectives in relative clauses, and it is well known that children acquire the facility to produce sentences with attributive adjectives, such as:

54. Where's my red wagon?

long before they are able to produce sentences with predicate adjectives in relative clauses, such as:

55. Where's my wagon that is red?

In fact, even to most adult speakers of English, sentences like 54 are fully grammatical and relatively common in speech, whereas those like 55 sound strange and are much less likely to be encountered in speech.

But these observations, although correct, do not undermine the view that attributive adjectives are obtained from relative clauses containing predicate adjectives via the whiz-deletion and adjective-preposing transformations. All they can be made to show is that, at some stage in the acquisition process, whiz deletion is taken to be an obligatory transformation that is later made optional (though perhaps still nearly obligatory whenever the remaining part of the relative clause upon application of whiz deletion is a single adjective). (For further consideration of whiz deletion and adjective preposing, see items 16–18.)

4. The Introduction of Nominal Expressions: The Replacement of Pronouns by Nouns

We are now in a position to give an account of how the entire content of nominal expressions is introduced into sentences. In Chapter 5, we maintained that there is a transformation that relates nominal expressions consisting simply of a noun (perhaps together with an article) to expressions consisting of a pronoun (or other expression that embodies the assumptions of the predicate in which the nominal expression plays some role) plus a relative clause. We did so in order to provide a syntactic account of the fact that sentences such as the following are stylistic variants:

56. Someone who is an expert will speak.
57. An expert will speak.

Taking example 56 as closer to the deep structure underlying these two sentences, we assume that 57 is obtained upon the application of (a) whiz deletion and (b) a rule that replaces the pronoun *someone* (which embodies the assumptions we have concerning the entities that play the role of agent of the verb *speak*) by the predicate nominal expression *an expert*.

But now, we are prepared to go one step further in uncovering the deep structure underlying examples like 56 and 57. Given what we have already said about relative-clause formation, we conclude that the deep structure in question is:

58. Someone is an expert. He will speak.

This conclusion is tantamount to the claim that where lexical content of nominal expressions is greater than what would be assumed of them given their role in a sentence, the content is introduced, as it were, from outside; that is, from other sentences.

†5. Some Restrictions on Relative-Clause Formation and Reduction

It turns out that there are definite limits on the complexity of the structures that can be converted into relative clauses in English, and there are also restrictions on what can be deleted by the various reduction transformations that we have considered so far, particularly whiz deletion. Some of these limits and restrictions are explored in this section.

It is, in general, possible to form sentences containing relative clauses in which the relative pronoun originates in a subordinate clause that functions as the object of a predicate. Thus, sentence 59 can be formed from the discourse 60:

59. The book that John thinks Bill hasn't read yet deals with the 1964 presidential campaign.
60. John thinks Bill hasn't read a certain book yet. It deals with the 1964 presidential campaign.

It is not possible, in standard English at least, to form sentences in which the relative pronoun originates in a non-extraposed subject clause, in a clause that is an object of a nonpredicate noun, or in another relative clause. These restrictions are illustrated by the following examples—first the underlying discourse is given; then the corresponding (appropriately asterisked) complex sentence:

61. That Bill hasn't read a certain book yet annoys John. It deals with the 1964 presidential campaign.
62.*The book that that Bill hasn't read yet annoys John deals with the 1964 presidential campaign.
63. I heard a rumor that the trustees were planning to fire a professor. He had offended some people by claiming that Theodore Roosevelt had been a Marxist.
64.*The professor whom I heard a rumor that the trustees were planning to fire had offended some people by claiming that Theodore Roosevelt had been a Marxist.
65. The doctor has just read a report that describes a certain patient's condition. He has been refusing food for the last two days.
66.*The patient whose condition the doctor has just read a report that describes has been refusing food for the last two days.

In addition, sentences cannot be formed if the relative pronoun originates as the subject of an object clause or extraposed subject clause unless the introductory word *that* has been deleted (for similar restrictions on the formation of questions, see items 22–25 of Chapter 3):

67. Mary thinks that a friend hasn't read the book yet. He doesn't have much time for such things.
68.*The friend who Mary thinks that hasn't read the book yet doesn't have much time for such things.
69. The friend who Mary thinks hasn't read the book yet doesn't have much time for such things.
70. It annoys Mary that a certain friend hasn't read the book yet.
71.*The friend who it annoys Mary that hasn't read the book yet doesn't have much time for such things.
72. ?The friend who it annoys Mary hasn't read the book yet doesn't have much time for such things.

Just to describe such restrictions is an almost overwhelming task; initial efforts were made by Lees in his *Grammar of English Nominalizations*, and a fairly systematic treatment is to be found in Chomsky's article "Current Issues in Linguistic Theory" in Fodor and Katz (eds.), *The Structure of Language*. The most thorough discussion is to be found in John R. Ross's M.I.T. doctoral dissertation, *Constraints on Variables in Syntax*, 1967, in which particular constraints on particular transformations are related to very general properties of constraints in universal grammar. But we still lack an explanation for the presence of these constraints in universal grammar, although it would seem that, among other things, they guarantee that the structures one obtains upon application of transformational rules are not mind-boggling, if the structures to which they apply are not already so (though at the end of Chapter 3, we saw that it is possible to form mind-boggling deep structures very easily).

Whiz deletion also has the very important restriction that to some extent the underlying form of the deleted verb *be* must be determinable from the context of the entire sentence. For example, the sentence:

73. I am teaching a class of highly intelligent students.

is a stylistic variant of:

74. I am teaching a class of students who *are* highly intelligent.

but not of:

75. I am teaching a class of students who *were* highly intelligent.
76. I am teaching a class of students who *will be* highly intelligent.

and so forth. The reason why the present-tense form of the verb *be* can be deleted to create 73, but not the past or future forms, is that the present-tense form is the expected form given that the main verb of the sentence is in the present tense. Similarly, the sentence:

77. I have listened to many dull nominating speeches.

is a stylistic variant of:

78. I have listened to many nominating speeches which *have been* dull.

This restriction on whiz deletion is also a consequence of a universal constraint on deletion transformations generally; the elements deleted must always be determinable from context (interpreted broadly, this can mean not only the context of the sentence itself, but the social and physical setting appropriate to the uttering of the sentence).

6. Transformations Relating to Sentence Types outside the Propositional Core: Interrogative Sentences

Having rejected the framework provided by early generative-transformational theory, we are now faced with the problems of determining the nature of deep structure representations of sentences outside the propositional core, and of formulating transformations to convert these into their proper surface structures. We tackle these problems first as they relate to interrogative sentences.

In their book *An Integrated Theory of Linguistic Descriptions*, Katz and Postal propose that every question in English should be analyzed as containing in its deep structure a special abstract element Q that acts as a "trigger" for the application of the interrogative transformation and that is semantically equivalent to the expression *I request you to tell me*. The deep structure underlying a question such as:

79. Are you coming?

therefore looks like:

80. Q you are coming.

and means the same as:

81. I request you to tell me whether you are coming.

Question-word interrogative sentences, moreover, are analyzed as containing an underlying indefinite pronoun prefixed by the abstract element *WH*. Thus, the deep structure underlying a question such as:

82. Who is coming?

looks like:

83. Q *WH* + someone is coming.

and means the same as:

84. I request you to tell me who is coming.

We shall follow Katz and Postal's analysis, except that we shall maintain that the element which introduces interrogative sentences is the expression *I request you to tell me*, and that the symbol Q is simply to be considered a convenient "abbreviation" to stand for that expression. We shall also consider the question-words to be special indefinite pronouns in their own right, and not complex entities made up of an abstract interrogative element plus the usual indefinite pronoun.

There are four parts to the interrogative transformation itself. First, the interrogative word is placed at the beginning of the clause containing it (in yes-no questions this is the word *whether*—the treatment of such sentences is discussed below). If there is more than one interrogative word in a clause, only one is brought forward. Second, the expression *I request you to tell me* is optionally deleted. Third, if this expression has been deleted, the first helping verb is moved to a position immediately following the question-word; if there is no helping verb, then the form of the verb *do* that is the same in tense and number as the main verb is put in that position, and the main verb loses its inflection (this aspect of the rule remains the same from our account in Chapter 3). Fourth, if Q has been deleted, then *whether* must be deleted.

The first part of this transformation can be applied independently of the other three in the formation of indirect questions such as:

85. John asked Bill whether Tom was coming.
86. The man wondered what could be done about the dent in his car's fender.

For this reason it is appropriate to say that there are two separate interrogative transformations. The first puts question-words at the beginning of the clauses in which they occur (this rule is identical in its effect with that part of the relative-clause-formation transformation which puts relative pronouns at the beginning of relative clauses—Katz and Postal in fact suggested that the interrogative and relative pronouns themselves be identified as being the same, but this is incorrect since the interrogative pronouns are indefinite whereas the relative pronouns are definite). The second interrogative transformation performs the other three operations just described.

Simple interrogative sentences are often followed by such expressions as *or not*, *or isn't he*, and so forth; for example:

87. Are you coming or not?
88. Are you coming or aren't you?

This is a consequence of the fact that simple interrogative sentences are always questions about alternatives (a fact which is nicely revealed by the Katz and Postal analysis of interrogative sentences), since the same expressions may also appear in the fuller stylistic variants of such sentences. For example:

89. I request you to tell me whether or not you are coming.
90. I request you to tell me whether you are coming or whether you aren't.

The additional expression need not be the negative version of the first part of the question either. Consider:

91. Are you coming or staying?
92. Do you want artichoke hearts or would you prefer buttered spinach?

Normally, the person who asks a simple question expects that the respondent will affirm the truth of one of the alternatives; in the case of 79, 87, and 88, the answers *yes* or *no* will do, whereas the expected answer to 91 is either *coming* or *staying*, and to 92 *artichoke hearts* or *buttered spinach*. Any other response would be an evasion of the question, or inappropriate, for example *maybe, God knows, there's a fly in your soup*, or silence. This suggests that the meaning of *whether . . . or* is that of the expression *which of the following is true*.

The present analysis of questions also explains the semantic oddity of first person questions such as:

93. Am I in the kitchen?

which are odd since a person generally knows where he is and it is strange to ask for information one already knows. Of course it is possible for someone not to know where he is, for example upon recovering consciousness, in which case questions such as 93 are not odd. Also it is not odd to ask questions about oneself in the past or future, for example:

94. Did I like kindergarten?

This is because the *I* of *I request you to tell me* is the *I* of the present, whereas the *I* of *I liked kindergarten* is the *I* of the past.

The present analysis, however, does not do justice to rhetorical questions, questions that do not call for a response from the addressee. The surface structure of a rhetorical question is no different from that of an ordinary question, so that a question such as:

95. Could the testimony you have just heard possibly be false?

could be rhetorical or not. We propose that the deep structure of rhetorical questions is like that of 96:

96. I request you to consider whether the testimony you have just heard could possibly be false.

and that the expression *I request you to consider* may be deleted just like the expression *I request you to tell me* discussed above.

Negative questions, such as 97 below, are especially problematic, because semantically they do not function as denials of questions, but rather they give an indication of what answer the questioner expects:

97. Aren't you coming?

We take up this matter in more detail in Section 10, which deals with the semantic and syntactic properties of negative sentences.

7. Imperative Sentences

The notion "imperative sentence" is actually not as clear as it might seem. If it is used as a syntactic label to designate sentences with an understood second-person subject and an uninflected verb, we find that a number of semantically quite distinct sorts of sentences are included, for example:

98. Close the door!
99. Look out for your head!
100. Have a good time at the party!
101. Win $1,000 in the new supermarket giveaway!
102. Bake for one hour at 350° F. for best results.
103. Remember when we last went to a drive-in movie?

From a semantic point of view, 98 expresses a command, 99 a warning, 100 a wish, 101 a promise (of sorts), 102 advice, and 103 a question. Alternatively, if we restrict the label to designate only one of these semantic types, say commands, we artificially exclude examples which are very similar semantically, and which are expressed identically in surface syntax. Moreover, there is a certain amount of overlap; 98 could be a warning as well as a command, and 99 could be a command as well as a warning. Finally, commands can be expressed syntactically in other ways, for example in the syntactic form of a question, as when a customer requests a cup of coffee with the utterance:

104. May I have a cup of coffee, please?

We conclude that "imperative sentence" as a syntactic label is the more useful.

Like interrogative sentences, the imperative sentences 98–103 have longer stylistic variants. They are:

105. I order you to close the door!
106. I warn you to look out for your head!
107. I hope that you have a good time at the party!
108. I promise you that you might win $1,000 in the new supermarket giveaway!
109. I advise you to bake for one hour at 350° F. for best results.
110. I ask you to remember when we last went to a drive-in movie.

In each of the examples 105–110 we can tell from examining the main verb what the sentence expresses—a command, a warning, a wish, a promise, advice, or a question—and we claim that the imperative sentences 98–103 are obtained from them by a deletion transformation. That transformation, which we call the imperative transformation, is capable of deleting any of the verbs *order, warn, wish, promise, advise, ask,* and perhaps a few others, together with its first-person-singular subject, second-person object, and either the word *to* that introduces a dependent infinitive or the string of words *that you might* that introduces a dependent subordinate clause.

Examples 81, 84, 89, 90, and 105–110 have the further interesting property of performing what their main verbs describe. Such sentences are called performative sentences, and the main verbs in them are called performative verbs, terms which are due to the Oxford philosopher J. L. Austin (see his book *How to Do Things with Words*). Not all performative sentences can be converted into imperative or interrogative sentences, however; consider for example:

111. I pronounce you man and wife.
112. I name this child Hortense.
113. I apologize for the nasty things I said to you yesterday.
114. I confess that I was lurking beneath your window yesterday.
115. I bet you that George wins the next race.
116. I affirm the intentions of this nation to intervene in any crisis which threatens its security.
117. I order Harry to appear before me at nine A.M. tomorrow.
118. I declare to you that Horace eats peas with a knife.

For a sentence to be a performative sentence, its deep-structure main verb must be a performative verb in the present tense, its subject must be first person (usually, but not necessarily, singular), and it must be affirmative. For this reason, none of the following are to be considered performative sentences:

119. I think that Horace eats peas with a knife.
120. I named this child Hortense.
121. John bets you that George wins the next race.
122. I don't pronounce you man and wife.

In 119, the main verb is not a performative verb; in 120 the main verb is not in the present tense; in 121 the subject is not first person; and in 122 the sentence is negative. It can be argued, however, that deeper analysis reveals every sentence in English to be a performative sentence of some sort. Interrogative and imperative sentences can be so designated, since, as we have asserted, the main verbs of their deep structures are performative verbs in the present tense, with first-person subjects. Similarly, declarative sentences can be viewed as arising from performative sentences which start out *I declare to you that*. In particular, 118 can be considered a stylistic variant of the ordinary declarative sentence:

123. Horace eats peas with a knife.

I shall not elaborate the arguments that support this contention, but instead refer the interested reader to an article by John R. Ross entitled "On Declarative Sentences," in Jacobs and Rosenbaum (eds.), *Readings in English Transformational Grammar*.

Negative imperative sentences, which may be warnings, promises, or prohibitions, such as:

124. Don't take chances with fire!
125. Don't think that you can get away with that!
126. Never suffer from tired blood again!

start out in deep structure looking like:

127. I warn you not to take chances with fire!
128. I order you not to think that you can get away with that!
129. I promise you that you will never suffer from tired blood again.

The class of performative verbs that can be deleted to form prohibitions is somewhat smaller than the corresponding class for ordinary imperative sentences; for example *hope* and *advise* are not deletable to form prohibitions. There are also some performative verbs, notably *prohibit* and *forbid*, which semantically incorporate the negation that is expressed in prohibitives. Thus, 130 below is a paraphrase of 124 and 127:

130. I forbid you to take chances with fire!

Sentence 130 itself cannot, of course, be converted syntactically into a prohibitive sentence.

8. Passive Sentences

The problem of describing the syntactic relation between active and passive sentences in English has probably received more attention from generative-transformational grammarians than any other single problem of English syntax, and numerous solutions have been proposed; see for example the three very different treatments by Chomsky in *Syntactic Structures*, *Aspects of the Theory of Syntax*, and "Remarks on Nominalization," as well as those proposed recently by Charles J. Fillmore in "The Case for Case" and by Kinsuke Hasegawa in "The Passive Construction in English." The description that we propose here is most similar to that of Fillmore's; our account differs from his only in a few details.

We suggest that in the passive sentences such as:

131. John was startled by a loud noise.
132. This house was lived in by George Washington.

the main predicates are the past participles *startled* and *lived*, which, like any adjectives, occur with a form of the verb *be*. The special thing about passive sentences is that the transformational rules which correlate subjects and objects operate somewhat differently on them; in particular, the expressions that designate the agent or the instrument roles are never made subject, but are always made oblique object. Generally, the expression which plays the patient role is made subject, as in 131.

Example 132, which is a repetition of example 39 of Chapter 3, illustrates a somewhat more complex situation. If we examine the core sentence that corresponds to example 132, namely:

133. George Washington lived in this house.

and ask what role is being played by the various nominal expressions in it, particularly the oblique object *this house*, we discover, I believe, that it is not only playing a locative role but also a patient role. It tells us not only where George Washington lived but also what he lived in. Therefore, as a patient, the expression *this house* can be made into the subject of the past participle *lived*, whereas the preposition which expresses its locative role is put after the verb. In contrast, the core sentences:

134. George Washington lived in Virginia.
135. George Washington remained in this house.

do not have grammatical passive counterparts, since *Virginia* cannot be a patient of *live in* (it is presumed to be unaffected by the action), and no object at all can be patient of *remain in*.

A puzzling fact, for which there appears to be no explanation under our account of the structure of passive sentences, is that the agent (or instrument) and patient of a passive sentence cannot refer to the same individual. Thus, although we can say both:

136. Mary surprised John.
137. John was surprised by Mary.

and we can say:

138. Mary surprised herself.

we find that the passive counterpart to 138 is ungrammatical:

139.*Mary was surprised by herself.

(This example is, of course, grammatical if *by herself* is taken to mean *all alone*, and not taken as an agent). But, while 139 is ungrammatical, we find that the following sentence is not:

140. Mary was surprised at herself.

The reason is that 140 is not a passive sentence at all; *surprised* there functions as a pure adjective, homophonous (same in pronounciation) with the past participle of the verb *surprise*. The role of *herself* in 140 is furthermore not that of agent, but that of stimulus. (See problems 28–29 for further consideration of the passive construction and related problems.)

9. Negative Sentences

The study of the semantic and syntactic properties of negation has been going on for millennia, largely because of the importance of the concept of negation for logic. In deference to the long history and tradition of the subject, we shall begin our discussion of negative sentences by considering an example taken from a seventeenth-century French logic textbook, *The Art of Thinking*, by Antoine Arnald:

141. Brutus didn't kill a tyrant.

The semantic interpretation of 141 is not particularly difficult, given the semantic interpretation of its affirmative counterpart:

142. Brutus killed a tyrant.

Example 141 is a denial of 142, and, semantically, the negative element of 141 can be thought of as a one-place predicate with the sentence 142 as its argument. Syntactically, however, it cannot be expressed in quite this way in English; we cannot say:

143.*That Brutus killed a tyrant is not.

Rather, the negative element occurs syntactically as an adverb which is placed in front of the main predicate in the clause which is its argument. As a result, negative sentences such as 141 are simple in their surface structures but complex in their deep structures.

To perceive more clearly the nature of the deep structure underlying 141, let us undo the effects of the relative-clause-formation transformation and adopt the logical notation developed in Chapter 3, which differs from the notation appropriate for deep structures only in that roles and assumptions are ignored. Doing this, we obtain:

144. Not [Brutus (x). Tyrant (y). Killed (x, y)]

That is, example 141 affirms that not all of the following assertions are true:

145. Someone killed someone.
146. The person who killed someone was Brutus.
147. The person whom someone killed was a tyrant.

According to a law of logic formulated by De Morgan in the nineteenth century, formula 144 is equivalent to the following expression:

148. Not [Brutus (x)]   or   Not [Tyrant (y)]   or
     Not [Killed (x, y)]

In other words, to affirm that not all the propositions 145–147 are true is to affirm that at least one of them is not true. This is what is expressed by 148, which in more or less ordinary English would read:

149. Either no one killed anyone, or the person who killed someone is not Brutus, or the person whom someone killed is not a tyrant.

But, as the reader should convince himself, one would affirm 141 just in case he would also be willing to affirm 149.

If a person wanted to use the surface syntactic form of 141, and yet indicate that a particular one of the three possibilities of 149 is true, he would emphasize the appropriate predicate in 141 by raising the pitch of his voice on the accented syllable of that predicate. Thus, if he wished to deny that Brutus was involved in any killing, he would say:

Bru
150.   tus didn't kill a tyrant.

If he wished to deny that the person killed was a tyrant, he would say:

ty
151. Brutus didn't kill a   rant.

Finally, if he wished to deny that any killing took place, he would say:

kill
152. Brutus didn't   a tyrant.

Besides formulating the law which states that, in general, the denial of a conjunction of propositions is equivalent to the denial of at least one of them, De Morgan also formulated the converse principle: the denial of a disjunction of propositions (propositions connected by *or*) is equivalent to the separate denial of each of them. As a consequence, 153 below is logically equivalent to 154:

153. It is not the case that the moon is made of green cheese or that storks bring babies.
154. The moon is not made of green cheese and storks do not bring babies.

This equivalence may explain the fact that a significantly greater number of Alligators used a plural pronoun in response to Walrus's statement in example 64 of Chapter 2:

155. Neither John nor Tom stayed.

than to that of 59 of Chapter 2:

156. Either John or Tom will stay.

since 155 is logically equivalent to:

157. John and Tom didn't stay.

Negative sentences are in general quite different semantically from propositional core sentences containing a negated predicate, such as *unhappy*. Compare, for example, the following sentences:

158. John is unhappy.
159. John isn't happy.

If for the moment we think of happiness as measured along a scale ranging from "unhappy" or "sad" at one end to "happy" at the other, then 158 affirms that John's feelings are at the "unhappy" end of the scale, and 159 affirms that they are not at the "happy" end. From this, however, it does not follow that in 159 they are necessarily at the "unhappy" end. Also, by De Morgan's Law, 159 could be used to affirm that the person who is happy is not John, whereas 158 could never be used to affirm this.

†10. More on Negative Sentences

Negative sentences which contain in their surface structures indefinite pronouns or quantifier words exhibit other syntactic complexities of various sorts. Let us begin by inquiring what the negative counterpart is to the following sentence:

160. John saw someone.

This example is ambiguous, depending upon whether *someone* is interpreted as an indefinite pronoun, or as meaning roughly *a particular person whose identity is not being revealed*. In the latter sense, *someone* starts out in deep structure as a predicate. It turns out that, under the first interpretation, 160 has two negative counterparts, namely:

161. John didn't see anyone.
162. John saw no one.

Examples 161 and 162 mean the same thing, and are each equivalent semantically to:

163. That John saw someone is not the case.

Under the second interpretation, 160 has the following negative counterpart:

164. John didn't see someone.

For clarity, let us italicize instances of predicate *someone* in our examples. If we do this, then we say that the negative counterparts of 160 are 161 and 162, and 164 is the negative counterpart of:

165. John saw *someone*.

Similarly, the negative counterparts of:

166. John ate something.

are:

167. John didn't eat anything.
168. John ate nothing.

whereas the negative counterpart of:

169. John ate *something*.

is:

170. John didn't eat *something*.

We conclude that there is a transformation in English which optionally combines the negative element with any indefinite pronoun that follows the main predicate in a sentence; the result of this combination is a negative indefinite pronoun such as *no one, nothing, or nowhere*. If the negative element is not combined with the indefinite pronoun, then the indefinite pronoun is expressed as an *any*-word, such as *anyone, anything*, or *anywhere*.

Now consider:

171. Someone saw John.

Unlike 160, example 171 has only one negative counterpart, namely:

172. No one saw John.

We find that the example that would correspond to 166 is ungrammatical:

173.*Anyone didn't see John.

On the other hand, the negative counterpart of:

174. *Someone* saw John.

is:

175. *Someone* didn't see John.

We observe that the negative element obligatorily combines with the indefinite pronoun that precedes the main predicate of a sentence. As a result, a sentence such as 176 below, which contains two surface indefinite pronouns, one a subject and one an object, has only one negative counterpart, namely 177:

176. Someone ate something.
177. No one ate anything.

Sentences containing quantified nominal expressions, that is, nominal expressions introduced by such words as *all, most, many, some, several, few*, or any expression designating a number or fraction, such as *one, ten, half, three-quarters*, and so forth, exhibit properties similar to sentences containing indefinite pronouns. Thus, like 160, example 178 below has two negative counterparts, 179 and 180:

178. John knows some of his classmates.
179. John doesn't know any of his classmates.
180. John knows none of his classmates.

Also, like 160, 178 is ambiguous, depending upon whether *some* is an indefinite quantifier or whether it has the meaning roughly of *a particular group*. As before, let us italicize the latter use of *some* in our examples. Then, the negative counterpart of 181 below is 182:

181. John knows *some* of his classmates.

182. John doesn't know *some* of his classmates.

Notice that unlike 178 and 179, examples 181 and 182 could both be true, just as 164 and 165 could both be true.
Now consider:

183. John knows many of his classmates.
184. John doesn't know many of his classmates.
185. John knows not many of his classmates.

Just as 179 and 180 are the negative counterparts of 178, so 184 and 185 are the negative counterparts of 183. But there is a further complication with examples 183–185. Example 183 is ambiguous in the same way that 178 is; *many* can be interpreted to mean either *a large group* or *a particular large group*. Again, let us italicize the latter use of *many*. If we ask what the negative counterpart is of the following example, however:

186. John knows *many* of his classmates.

we observe that it is:

187. John doesn't know *many* of his classmates.

But, observe that 187 has the same surface form as 184; that is, 184 is ambiguous in the same way that 183 is.

If we now substitute the word *all* for *many* in 183, we notice that the resulting sentence 188 is unambiguous (since the expression *all of his classmates* necessarily designates a particular group):

188. John knows all of his classmates.

Consequently, the negative counterparts of 188 are also unambiguous:

189. John doesn't know all of his classmates.
190. John knows not all of his classmates.

We now consider examples in which the subject expression is quantified:

191. Some of his classmates know John.
192. Many of his classmates know John.
193. All of his classmates know John.

The negative counterparts of 191–193 are, respectively:

194. None of his classmates know John.
195. Not many of his classmates know John.
196. Not all of his classmates know John.

On the other hand, the negative counterparts of:

197. *Some* of his classmates know John.
198. *Many* of his classmates know John.

are, respectively:

199. *Some* of his classmates don't know John.
200. *Many* of his classmates don't know John.

And, since example 193 is unambiguous, we should expect that 201 below is a stylistic variant of 196, if it is grammatical:

201. All of his classmates don't know John.

Many persons find examples like 201 perfectly grammatical, but to others they are marginal or even downright ungrammatical. Finally, of those who do find them grammatical, there are apparently some who consider them not to be stylistic variants of sentences like 196, but rather of sentences like 194. I have no explanation for this.

It should be clear from the foregoing account that the syntax of negation in English is quite complex. In addition, there are many other problems concerning negation that we have not touched on here. (Some of these are taken up in items 32–34 at the end of this chapter.) We conclude this section with some remarks about negative interrogative sentences.

At the end of the section on interrogative sentences, we noted that negative questions, such as 202, are problematic:

202. Aren't you coming?

If we compare these with affirmative questions, such as 203:

203. Are you coming?

we notice that one asks a negative question if one expects that the answer to the corresponding affirmative question will be "yes." This is true whether the negative element is expressed as an adverb modifying the verb, as in 202, or combined with an indefinite pronoun somewhere in the sentence, as in the following examples:

204. Will no one help me with these packages?
205. Do you have no bananas?

The speaker of 204 clearly expects someone to help him, and the speaker of 205 expects the addressee to have some bananas. Notice also that a "yes" answer to questions like 205 is unclear. The literal affirmative answer to 205 would be 206 below, while if the addressee answers the corresponding affirmative question affirmatively, he would give 207:

206. Yes, we have no bananas.
207. Yes, we have some bananas.

While the facts concerning negative questions are clear, I have no clear explanation for them; that is to say, I cannot give a convincing reason why one uses negative questions like 202, 204 and 205 when one expects that the answer to the corresponding affirmative question will be "yes." If we ask what the deep structures for questions such as 202 look like, we come up with:

208. I request you to tell me whether you aren't coming.

Recalling that simple interrogative questions are questions about alternatives, we notice that in 208 and in 202 the affirmative alternative has been deleted, not the negative one, as in 203 and 209:

209. I request you to tell me whether you are coming.

This means that in the deep structure underlying 202, the

negative alternative has been placed first and the affrmative alternative second; that is, the deep structure is not 208, but rather 210:

> 210. I request you to tell me whether you aren't coming or whether you are coming.

Now, it is unusual in speech to place a negative alternative before an affirmative one, so perhaps when this device is used in the construction of interrogative sentences, it signals the expectation on the part of the speaker that the answer will be "yes." I make this proposal diffidently, however, since it is very possible that there is some deeper explanation.

11. The Movement of Relative and Content Clauses

We have concluded our discussion of the transformational account of the structure of the types of sentence outside the propositional core. Before going on to deal with the transformational apparatus required to handle the selection and placement of the various roles as subject, direct object, and oblique object, we shall present an analysis of the various transformational operations that are permitted on relative and content clauses. We do this because the nature of the phenomena is such that the ability of transformational theory to deal with them is particularly striking.

Earlier in this chapter, we indicated that there is a rule called the relative-clause-movement transformation that permits the shifting of a relative clause modifying a noun to the end of the sentence in which it occurs. Sentences 11 and 12 were given to illustrate the effect of the transformation. We repeat:

> 211. The man who was supposed to introduce the speaker hasn't arrived yet.
> 212. The man hasn't arrived yet who was supposed to introduce the speaker.

The stylistic significance of this transformation is particularly clear: It reduces the apparent complexity of the surface subject of the sentence, and so enables a speaker or writer to compose a sentence with a conceptually complex subject without having to burden his listener or reader with a lot of material in front of the main verb.

Other movement transformations in English have much the same effect. Compare the sentences:

213. Fears that the ship would sink mounted.
214. Fears mounted that the ship would sink.

In example 213, the clause *that the ship would sink* is not a relative clause, since there is no occurrence of a nominal expression coreferential with *fears* in its underlying structure (also note that the relative pronoun *which* cannot be inadvertently substituted for the particle *that* in 213). Rather, it is a content clause functioning as "object" of the noun *fears*, just as the corresponding clause in sentence 215 below is an object of the verb *fear*:

215. The captain feared that the ship would sink.

Nevertheless, the clause can be moved to the end of the entire sentence, as 214 illustrates, just as relative clauses can.

Finally, consider the sentences:

216. That the ship will sink is apparent to everyone on board.
217. It is apparent to everyone on board that the ship will sink.

In example 216, the content clause *that the ship will sink* simply is the subject of the sentence. Upon movement of that clause to the end of the sentence, by a transformational rule already referred to as extraposition, the pronoun *it* is made to stand as the surface-structure subject of the sentence.

Unlike the transformations that move relative and noun-object clauses to the end of the sentence, the extraposition transformation is, under certain circumstances, obligatory.

Thus, although we do have sentences such as:

218. It seems that the disorder is beginning to get out of hand.

in which the subject content clause *that the disorder is beginning to get out of hand* has been moved to the end of the sentence, it is ungrammatical to leave the content clause in subject position:

219.*That the disorder is beginning to get out of hand seems.

Besides having the desirable stylistic effect that we have already mentioned, the extraposition transformation is capable of converting certain sorts of structures which in and of themselves would be unintelligible into intelligible structures. Some consideration of this matter is to be found in item 32 of Chapter 3.

12. Limitations on the Movement of Content Clauses

The extraposition transformation is inapplicable, however, where applying it would move one content clause around another; for example, the rule is inapplicable to the following sentence:

220. That the sun is shining means that it's not likely to rain.

since the result of applying it is ungrammatical:

221.*It means that it's not likely to rain that the sun is shining.

The reason for this restriction is clear; the results of the application of the extraposition transformation to sentences like 220 are more complex perceptually than the original sentences. On the other hand, extraposition of a content clause around a relative clause does not create the type of perceptual complexity that 221 exhibits; therefore there should be, and in fact is, no restriction on extraposition around relative clauses:

222. That the ship would sink was apparent to everyone who noticed that the rats were deserting the deck.
223. It was apparent to everyone who noticed that the rats were deserting the deck that the ship would sink.

The movement of noun-object clauses is similarly restricted.

The applicability of the relative-clause-movement transformation is also limited, but in this case it is to prevent the creation of potential ambiguity. Consider the sentence:

224. A man whom I disliked spoke to a neighbor.

The application of the relative-clause-movement transformation to 224 would create the sentence:

225. A man spoke to a neighbor whom I disliked.

But this sentence would never be used, or understood, to mean what 224 means; rather, the relative clause *whom I disliked* would automatically be taken to modify the object noun *neighbor*. Therefore, we conclude that the relative-clause-movement transformation is inapplicable to sentences like 224, in which the clause, if moved, would be taken to modify another noun in the sentence.

13. The Formation of Infinitive Clauses

We turn now to a consideration of infinitive clauses, for example the expression *to win the election* in the following sentence:

226. Rocky expects to win the election.

Once we have determined the syntactic rules that govern the formation of infinitive clauses in English, we will be in a position to account for the syntactic properties of helping verbs, and of tenses of verbs (which will be considered in the next section). It will also be possible to generalize these rules to account for the properties of gerundive clauses, such as the expression *winning the election* in 227:

227. Winning the election was easy for Rocky.

but we shall not take this matter up here.

Example 226 is a stylistic variant of the following sentence:

228. Rocky expects that he will win the election.

If we consider the structure that 228 represents to be more basic than that which 226 represents, it follows that there is an infinitive-formation transformation in English that has the following effect: (a) it deletes the subject of the underlying finite clause and the introductory particle *that*, (b) it deletes certain helping verbs, such as *will*, from the underlying finite clause, and (c) it inserts the element *to* in front of the main verb of the clause. The rule, moreover, is optional, since both 226 and 228 are fully grammatical.

There are, however, sentences in which the application is obligatory. Consider for example:

229. Rocky wants to win the election.
230. Rocky is trying to win the election.

In standard English, at least, 229 and 230 do not have grammatical counterparts containing finite clauses; that is, we do not accept as grammatical such sentences as:

231.*Rocky wants that he should win the election.
232.*Rocky is trying that he might win the election.

Sentences like 231 are common, however, in nonstandard English, which suggests that while the rule is obligatory in standard English when the main verb of the sentence is *want* or *try* it is optional in certain nonstandard dialects, at least when the main verb is *want*.

In 228, the finite-clause object of the main predicate *expects* is playing the role of patient of that particular predicate. Upon application of the infinitive-clause-formation transformation, the resulting infinitive clause continues as the syntactic object of *expects.* In 228, moreover, the subject of the object finite clause refers to the same entity as the subject of *expects.* Let us now consider an example in which the subject of the object clause refers to a different entity:

233. Rocky expects that Dick will win the election.

This sentence also has a stylistic variant in which the infinitive clause *to win the election* appears; however, the sentence differs from 226. It is:

234. Rocky expects Dick to win the election.

In 234, the nominal expression *Dick* has become the direct object of the verb *expects* and has been removed from the subordinate clause from which it originally came. To see what has happened, let us consider tree diagrams (Figures 6 and 7) of the surface structures of sentences 233 and 234.[1] The infinitive-formation transformation copies the subject of the underlying finite subordinate clause as the direct object of the main clause, and then the subject of the subordinate clause is deleted.

To understand why the subject of the subordinate clause must be thought of as having become the object of the main clause, consider the following sentence, which is the passive counterpart to 234:

235. Dick is expected by Rocky to win the election.

We have already seen, in our section on passive sentences, that passive sentences are only possible if the corresponding active sentences contain objects that are the same as the subjects of the passive sentences. In particular, we would expect 235 to be grammatical only if the expression, *Dick,* which is its subject, is the object of 234.

There is another reason for considering that the subject

---

[1] For key to abbreviations in these and the following figures, see legend accompanying Figure 5, page 109.

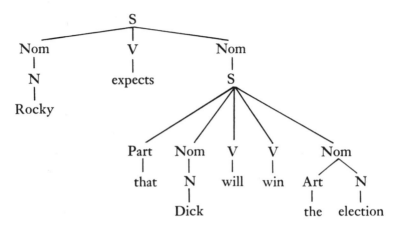

Figure 6. Surface structure of example 233.

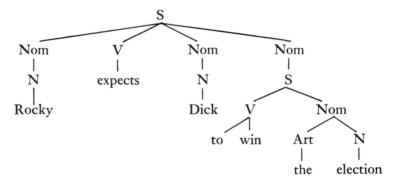

Figure 7. Surface structure of example 234.

of the underlying subordinate clause becomes the object of the main clause upon application of the infinitive-formation transformation. Consider once again sentences 226 and 228:

226. Rocky expects to win the election.
228. Rocky expects that he will win the election.

If the infinitive-formation transformation first copies the subject of the subordinate clause as object of the main clause, and then deletes the subject of the subordinate clause, the result would not be 226, but rather 236:

236. Rocky expects himself to win the election.

That is, the subject of the subordinate clause, having been copied as the object of the main clause, should become a reflexive pronoun, in accordance with our discussion in Chapter 5, Section 4. But 236 is a grammatical sentence, and is furthermore a stylistic variant of both 226 and 228. Therefore, we require, besides the infinitive-formation transformation, another rule which, in this case, optionally deletes the reflexive-pronoun object. Let us call this the reflexive-object-deletion transformation.

The reflexive-object-deletion transformation is optional when the main verb of the main clause is *expect* or *want*; it is obligatory when the main verb happens to be *try*. Thus, 237 below, in which the main verb is *want*, is grammatical, whereas 238 is ungrammatical:

237. I want myself to look handsome.
238.*I am trying myself to look handsome.

The rule is inapplicable when the verb of the main clause is *think*; consider the following examples:

239. John thinks that he is honest.
240. John thinks himself to be honest.
241.*John thinks to be honest.

On the other hand, there is another transformation which is optionally applicable to the structure represented by 240, a rule which deletes the expression *to be*. If applied, it results in the following stylistic variant of 239 and 240:

242. John thinks himself honest.

We refer to this rule simply as the *to-be*-deletion transformation.

The infinitive-formation transformation may itself be inapplicable, depending upon the choice of main verb. For example, the following sentence 243 has no stylistic variant in which an infinitive clause appears:

243. The little boy hinted that he was tired.
244.*The little boy hinted himself to be tired.
245.*The little boy hinted himself tired.
246.*The little boy hinted to be tired.
247.*The little boy hinted tired.

As 244–247 indicate, it is impossible to "save" the grammaticality of any sentence containing the main verb *hint*, in which the object clause has been turned into an infinitive. Finally, there are verbs which permit their object clauses to be turned into infinitives only when the verb in the subordinate clause is one of a certain set of verbs; for example, the verb *think* (when not itself passive) permits infinitive-clause formation only when the subordinate clause has *be* as its main verb. Thus, while 240 is grammatical, 248 below is not:

248.*John thinks Harry to like artichoke hearts.

The infinitive-formation transformation is not permitted to form sentences like 248; the deep structures underlying them can only be expressed with finite object clauses, for example:

249. John thinks that Harry likes artichoke hearts.

Thus far in our consideration of infinitive-clause formation, we have dealt only with clauses functioning as objects of predicates; infinitive clauses, however, also occur as subjects, as in the sentence:

250. For John to go is impossible.

Example 250 is itself a stylistic variant of the sentence:

251. That John will go is impossible.

We may therefore conclude that the infinitive clause in 250 is created by the infinitive-formation transformation from the finite clause in 251. However, the subject of that clause, instead of being copied as the object of the main predicate in the main clause, remains inside the subordinate clause, and the preposition *for* is inserted in front of it. The surface structures of 250 and 251 may be diagrammed as in Figures 8 and 9.

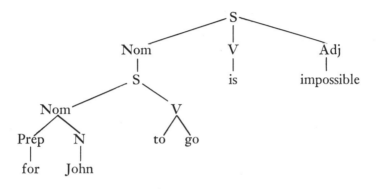

Figure 8.   Surface structure of example 250.

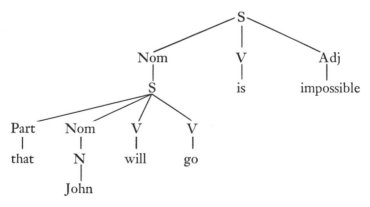

Figure 9.   Surface structure of example 251.

The structures underlying 250 and 251 also may undergo the extraposition transformation, resulting in:

252. It is impossible for John to go.
253. It is impossible that John will go.

Like *impossible*, the predicate adjective *unlikely* can be used with a finite subject clause; compare 251 and 253 with the following examples:

254. That John will go is certain.
255. It is certain that John will go.

Unlike *impossible*, however, *certain* does not occur normally with infinitive clause subjects; the following examples strike me as marginally grammatical at best:

256.*For John to go is certain.
257.*It is certain for John to go.

Rather, we find that examples 254 and 255 have, as a stylistic variant, the following sentence:

258. John is certain to go.

The subject of the subordinate clause has been made into the subject of the main clause, and the remaining part of the clause has been placed after the main predicate *certain*. In other words, the underlying subject clause has been "split"; part of it has been converted into the surface subject of the main predicate, and the remainder has been converted into a surface object of the main predicate. Compare Figures 10 and 11, in which the surface structures of examples 254 and 258 are diagrammed.

This splitting apart of the underlying clause can be described as resulting from the following operations: (a) copying the subject of the subordinate clause as subject of the main clause, (b) deleting the subject of the subordinate clause, (c) deleting such helping verbs as *will*, and the introductory word *that*, (d) inserting *to* in front of the main verb of the subordinate clause, (e) copying the clause as object of the main predicate, and (f) deleting the original occurrence of the clause. The

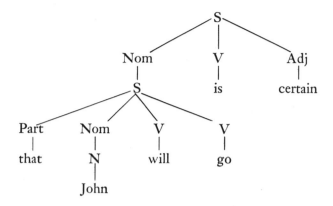

Figure 10.   Surface structure of example 254.

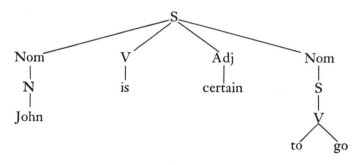

Figure 11.   Surface structure of example 258.

step-by-step character of these operations is illustrated in Figure 12 on page 183.

Thus, the infinitive-formation transformation can operate in two different ways on a subject clause, and the choice is dependent upon its predicate. If the predicate happens to be *impossible*, then the clause will remain intact and the resulting infinitive will function as a whole as the subject of that predicate, as in example 250:

250. For John to go is impossible.

If the predicate happens to be *certain*, then the clause will be split apart, the subject being made into the surface subject of the main predicate, and the remaining part of the clause being made into its surface object, as in example 258:

258. John is certain to go.

It turns out that there are only a handful of predicate adjectives that, like *certain*, require the splitting of their subject clause for infinitive-clause formation (among them *likely*, *unlikely*, *sure*). The great majority of predicate adjectives that permit infinitive-clause formation of their subject clauses behave like *impossible* (*common*, *uncommon*, *legal*, *illegal*).

Among verbs that occur with subject clauses that may be made into infinitives, the following require splitting: *seem*, *appear*, *happen*, and *turn out*. As a result, the following examples are stylistic variants (note that if the infinitive-formation transformation is not applied to sentences containing main verbs of this class, then the extraposition transformation must be applied):

259. It appears to me that John has worked out a solution to his problems.
260. John appears to me to have worked out a solution to his problems.

The *to-be*-deletion transformation is optionally applicable when the main verb is *seem* or *appear*, but not when it is *happen*. Thus, 261 and 262 below are stylistic variants, but while 263 is grammatical, 264 is not:

261. That John needs medical attention seems to me to be clear.
262. That John needs medical attention seems clear to me.
263. John happens to be extremely wealthy.

Figure 12.   (Opposite) Step-by-step operation of the infinitive formation and splitting transformation.

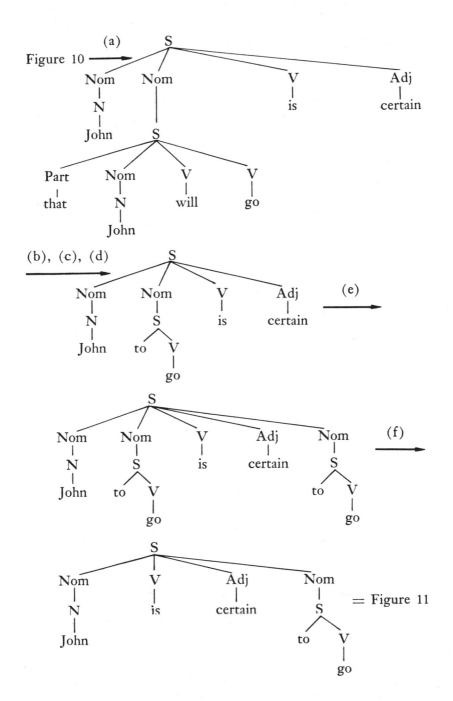

264.*John happens extremely wealthy.

On the other hand, the following verbs, which also permit their subject clauses to be converted into infinitives, require that the infinitive clause as a whole remain subject (that is, it cannot undergo splitting): *annoy*, *disturb*, *excite*, and *please* (there are many others as well). Thus the following are all stylistic variants:

265. That John hasn't done his homework yet annoys me.
266. It annoys me that John hasn't done his homework yet.
267. For John not to have done his homework yet annoys me.
268. It annoys me for John not to have done his homework yet.

Finally, when a finite object clause is accompanied by another object, the infinitive-formation transformation may apply provided that the subject of the clause refers to the same entity as the other object. Thus the sentence:

269. John told Mary that she should telephone Bill immediately.

has a stylistic variant:

270. John told Mary to telephone Bill immediately.

since the subject of the finite clause, *she*, refers to the same person as the object of the verb *tell*, *Mary*. But the infinitive formation transformation cannot be applied to the structure underlying the sentence:

271. John told Mary that Bill should telephone Stanley immediately.

If it is applied, the result is ungrammatical:

272.*John told Mary (for) Bill to telephone Stanley immediately.

Some verbs, for example *force* and *compel*, require that the subject of their object clause be identical to their other object, and that the infinitive-formation transformation be applied. Example 273 below is grammatical; 274 and 275 are not:

273. The prosecuting attorney forced the witness to admit that he could not remember what time the crime was committed.
274. *The prosecuting attorney forced the witness that he admitted that he could not remember what time the crime was committed.
275. *The prosecuting attorney forced the witness that John admitted that he could not remember what time the crime was committed.

There are also a few verbs, including *promise*, that permit the infinitive-formation transformation to apply when the subject of the object clause refers to the same entity as the subject of the main clause, not the other object. Thus, 276 below is a stylistic variant of 277 but not of 278:

276. John promised Mary to meet Bill after class.
277. John promised Mary that he would meet Bill after class.
278. John promised Mary that she would meet Bill after class.

In this connection, it is interesting to note that the sentence:

279. Mary asked the chairman to be recognized.

is a stylistic variant of:

280. Mary asked the chairman that she be recognized.

whereas the sentence:

281. Mary asked the chairman to recognize her.

is a variant of:

282. Mary asked the chairman that he recognize her.

I have no explanation for this fact.

†14. The Syntactic Analysis of Some Helping Verbs and of Tense

If we compare the sentences:

283. The guards permitted no one to enter the auditorium.
284. The guards let no one enter the auditorium.

we notice that the infinitive-clause object of *let*, unlike that of *permit*, is not introduced by the word *to*. Traditionally, such clauses are called unmarked infinitives. (Other verbs that occur with unmarked infinitives include *make*, *have*, and certain verbs of perception such as *see*, *watch*, *hear*, *listen*, *notice*, and *feel*.) Moreover, according to traditional grammar, the constructions that follow the so-called modal helping verbs— that is, *can*, *could*, *may*, *might*, *must*, *shall*, *should*, *will*, and *would* (there is one other modal helping verb, *ought*, which takes an unmarked infinitive only when negated and not always even then)—are also considered to be unmarked infinitives. In the following example, the unmarked-infinitive clause occurring with the modal verb *may* is italicized:

285. Children may *feed the animals*.

In order to determine the deep structure underlying 285, we must provide a clear account of its meaning. The sentence is, in fact, ambiguous; it may be paraphrased by either 286 or 287:

286. It is possible that children will feed the animals.
287. It is permitted for children to feed the animals.

In other words, the modal verb *may* can be used to convey the sense of either the adjective *possible* or the passive of the verb *permit*. In both cases it is a one-place predicate which takes a clause as its subject, and if we now examine 285 again, we see that the clause must be converted to the infinitive and that it must be split.

The potential ambiguity of the modal verb *may* is a source for feeble jokes, such as the following:

288. A: The sign says that if you get too close, the animals may eat your buttons.
     B: It's a good thing they can't read.

Some other modal verbs also admit of two or more interpretations. *Must*, for example, can be interpreted to have the sense of either *necessary* or *certain*, as in the sentence:

289. The baby must eat what is good for him.

which is interpretable as either:

290. It is necessary that the baby eat what is good for him.

or:

291. It is certain that the baby eats what is good for him.

Should can be used to mean either *likely* or *obliged*, as in the sentence:

292. John should settle down and get married this year.

which can be interpreted to mean either of the following:

293. John is likely to settle down and get married this year.
294. John would be wise to settle down and get married this year.

If a modal verb has two senses, note that one sense has to do with probability of future occurrence (*possible, likely, certain*), and the other with morality and social judgment (*permitted, wise, necessary*). Only the modal verb *might*, and in very correct standard English *can*, have just one sense; *might* is used only in the sense of *possible*, as in the sentence:

295. Children might feed the animals.

which is interpretable only as 286, not as 287. Similarly, in very correct English, the sentence:

296. Children can feed the animals.

means only:

297. Children are able to feed the animals.

although the sense of 287 may be ascribed to it in less correct, though still standard, English.

The modal verb *will* is of special interest, since according to traditional grammar, it is used to express simple future tense, as in the sentence:

298. John will take the medicine.

It is not possible to paraphrase 298 in the manner in which we were able to paraphrase other sentences containing modal verbs, such as 285, 289, 292, 295, and 296. If we reflect on its meaning, however, it becomes clear that *will* is a one-place predicate whose subject is a clause in which the verb is not inflected for tense. The tense is supplied by *will* itself. That is, the deep structure of 298 is that shown in Figure 13.

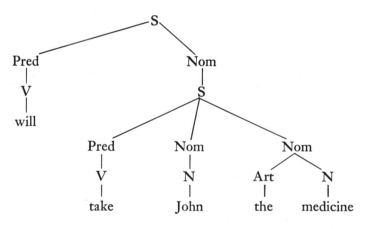

Figure 13.   Deep structure of example 298 (omitting roles).

To obtain the surface structure of 298 from the deep structure given in Figure 13, we need only apply the rules that make the clause the subject, and that then convert to the infinitive and split the clause. The infinitive-formation transformation, moreover, need delete nothing from the underlying clause except for the introductory word *that*.

Besides the simple future interpretation given in Figure 13, example 298 has two other interpretations (except in formal English, in which the *shall-will* distinction is maintained):

299. John resolves that he will take the medicine.
300. I resolve that John will take the medicine.

The *will* which appears in each of these paraphrases is, of course, the simple future *will*; otherwise 299, for example, could also mean:

301. John resolves that he will resolve that he will take the medicine.

and so on, ad infinitum.

If future tense is considered to be a one-place predicate whose argument is a clause, can the same be said of present and past tense? In such sentences as:

302. John appreciates your help.
303. John appreciated your help.

it seems eminently reasonable to provide the deep structures indicated in Figures 14 and 15 on page 190. In these figures, the symbols PRESENT and PAST abstractly represent the elements that generally turn up in surface structures as suffixes on verbs. When the infinitive-formation transformation is applied to the structures in Figures 14 and 15, the clause is split, and the main predicate is suffixed to the predicate of the underlying subordinate clause.

Since it is impossible to construct an English sentence without mentioning tense, it follows that in every deep structure there is at least one occurrence of a tense predicate, either past, present, or future. Moreover, the various surface tenses, particularly present, cover a wide range of semantic distinctions. The surface present tense of 302 corresponds to

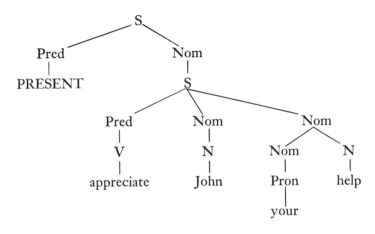

Figure 14.   Deep structure of example 302 (omitting roles).

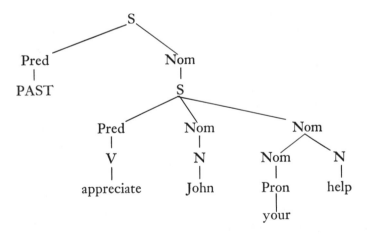

Figure 15.   Deep structure of example 303 (omitting roles).

a deep-structure present-tense predicate; in examples 304 and 305 below, the surface present tense corresponds to other deep-structure entities:

304. The plane lands tomorrow.
305. A mirror reflects light.

In the 304, the surface present tense expresses a deep-structure future-tense predicate, and in 305 it expresses a deep-structure timeless predicate; such sentences are called generic.

15. The Creation of Subjects and Objects

In Chapter 4 it was argued that for a given predicate, the selection of a particular nominal expression to be realized as, say, subject depends on the role structure of that predicate. It was also argued that the selection is governed by rules of considerable generality. In this section, we shall attempt to state precisely what is meant when we say that a particular nominal expression has been made subject or object.

Characteristically, the subject of a sentence is put directly in front of the main predicate, and it loses whatever preposition it might otherwise have had to indicate its role. Moreover, it has been the tradition to assume that the subject of the sentence forms a separate constituent from the remainder of the sentence; that is, that the parsing of a sentence such as:

306. The baby dislikes spinach.

is like that given in Figure 16. The traditional name given to the constituent indicated by question mark in Figure 16 is

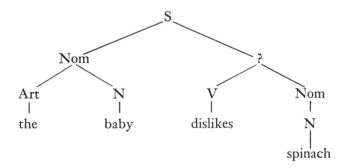

Figure 16.   Surface structure of example 306 in accordance with grammatical tradition.

"predicate"; in most generative-grammatical treatments, it is called "verb phrase" (abbreviated VP). Whatever label we ultimately decide to settle on for this constituent, however, it follows that if we accept the traditional assumption, the transformational rule that creates objects also must be assumed to create this constituent.

In many discussions, the subject of a sentence is identified further as its "topic," what the sentence is about. This identification is a bit misleading; as we have seen, the choice of the nominal expression to be made the subject is automatic, and that choice need not reflect the speaker's intentions concerning what a sentence is about. However, there are other syntactic devices in English for topicalizing a nominal expression in a sentence; interestingly, these devices typically involve putting the topicalized expression at or near the beginning of the sentence. Consider, for example, the following versions of 306, in which the direct object has been topicalized:

307. Spinach the baby dislikes.
308. Spinach, the baby dislikes it.
309. It's spinach that the baby dislikes.

In 307, the direct object has simply been shifted to sentence initial position, and it may be assumed that no new constituent has been created in the process. In 308, the topicalized object stands, as it were, in apposition to the sentence as a whole, so that the surface structure of 308 is to be analyzed as a sentence consisting of a nominal (*spinach*) and an entire sentence (*the baby dislikes it*) as constituents. Example 309 differs from 307 and 308 in that its deep structure is different from that of 306. In 309, *spinach* occurs as a predicate noun, and its subject is *that the baby dislikes*, which in turn is a reduction of *that* (or *the thing*) *which the baby dislikes*. This sentential form provides a very handy means for topicalizing almost any nominal expression, including those with prepositions. Consider, for example:

310. It was in Concord that the shot heard round the world was fired.

311. It's with weapons like this that the enemy intends to overrun us.

Unlike the creation of subjects, the creation of objects, both direct and oblique, presents no problem with regard to constituent analysis. There are, however, problems concerning their order relative to one another. For example, as was pointed out in item 23 of Chapter 4, there are verbs in English which take two objects, one of which must be direct and the other oblique, such that the nominal expression for either role may be made direct object. One such verb is *load*, as the following sentences illustrate (these are examples 180 and 181 of Chapter 4):

312. The driver loaded furniture onto the truck.
313. The driver loaded the truck with furniture.

Does this mean that we are free to make either of the roles illustrated by *with furniture* and *onto the truck* in 312 and 313 the direct object of *load*, or does the selection depend on the particular meaning of the verb? As we suggest in that problem, there is reason to believe that it depends on the meaning of the verb.

The following sentences have two oblique objects of the verb *speak* in different order. Is there any reason to believe that one or the other order is basic?

314. Sam spoke with Martha about Sheila.
315. Sam spoke about Sheila with Martha.

The answer, again, is yes, although the evidence, recently discovered by Paul Postal, is fairly indirect. Suppose we make the nominal expressions in the two oblique objects coreferential. It turns out that only sentences corresponding to the order shown in example 314 are grammatical:

316. Sam spoke with Martha about herself.
317.*Sam spoke about Martha with herself.

As Postal has shown, there is a principle of grammar that prevents any transformational rule from moving one nominal expression around another that is coreferential to it (under certain conditions, which need not concern us here). Suppose we assume that the rules which create and fix the relative order of oblique objects put *with*-objects before *about*-objects, and that there is a later optional-transformational rule which interchanges them when the two object nominals are not coreferential. In this way, we account for the grammaticality of 314–316 and the ungrammaticality of 317. The latter is ungrammatical because the transformation which interchanges the two oblique objects would move a nominal expression around another one coreferential to it.

A similar argument can be used to maintain that direct objects are put before indirect objects, as in the sentence:

318. John's mother sent a package of cookies to him.

and that sentences in which the indirect object immediately follows the verb (having also had its preposition deleted), such as 319, are derived by the further application of a transformational rule:

319. John's mother sent him a package of cookies.

A number of interesting, and some unsolved, problems concerning the rules for selecting subject and objects remain. See problems 39–40 for consideration of some of these.

PROBLEMS AND SUGGESTIONS FOR FURTHER STUDY

1. A number of recent articles and books provide reasonably helpful introductions to transformational analysis. See in particular Jerrold J. Katz, *The Philosophy of Language;* Ronald Langacker, *Language and Its Structure*, Chapter 5; D. Terence Langendoen, *The Study of Syntax*, Chapter 5; John Lyons, *Introduction to Theoretical Linguistics*, Chapters 6–8; Paul Postal, "Underlying and Superficial Linguistic Structure," in J. A. Emig, J. T. Fleming, and H. M. Popp (eds.), *Language and Learning*; and Peter S. Rosenbaum and Roderick Jacobs, *English Transformational Grammar*. Also see Noam Chomsky, "On the Notion 'Rule of Grammar,' " in J. A. Fodor and J. J. Katz (eds.), *The Structure of Language*, for discussion of the formal representation of transformational rules.

2. For discussion of the particle-movement transformation, see Bruce Fraser, "Some Remarks on the Verb-Particle

Construction in English," in F. P. Dinneen (ed.), *Monograph Series on Languages and Linguistics*, No. 19.

3. Many of the particles that enter into the verb-particle construction have directional "force" and often are identical with the prepositions associated with directional roles. Compare, for example, the sentences:

320. John brushed the lint off.
321. John brushed the lint off his suit.

Why is it reasonable to suppose that 320 is derived transformationally from a deep structure in which *off* appears as a preposition introducing an unspecified nominal expression (the nominal expression being deleted by the transformation)? But if so, why would there then have to be another particle-movement transformation in English that moves particles next to the main verb rather than away from it?

4. Other particles that enter into the verb-particle construction have completive "force"; compare the sentences:

322. John tore the manuscript.
323. John tore the manuscript up.

Why are such particles not to be derived from prepositions which introduce unspecified nominal expressions? Account for the lack of semantic contrast between the sentences:

324. The fire burned the house up.
325. The fire burned the house down.

and for the ungrammaticality of 327:

326. The fire burned the paper up.
327.*The fire burned the paper down.

5. In what respects is the syntactic behavior of adverbs such as *alone* and *around* similar to that of particles, and in what respects is it different?

6. Compare the movement of particles around nominal expressions with their movement around adverbs. Consider, for example, such sentences as:

   328. The dog trotted by slowly.
   329. The dog trotted slowly by.
   330. The dog trotted by so slowly that the camera was always able to keep it in focus.
   331.*The dog trotted so slowly that the camera was always able to keep it in focus by.
   332. ?The dog trotted so slowly by that the camera was always able to keep it in focus.

7. Why is the clause-introducing element *that* always deletable when the clause functions as an object of a noun such as *fact* or *possibility*? Compare example 22 with the following:

   333. The possibility he will forfeit his bond seems quite certain.

8. The relative pronoun that stands for the subject of the relative clause cannot be deleted in standard English if it modifies an object nominal, as the following examples illustrate:

   334. I admire the people who directed the rescue operations.
   335. I admire the people that directed the rescue operations.
   336.*I admire the people directed the rescue operations.

Show that this restriction does not follow from the perceptual strategy discussed in Section 2. Can you think of any reasons for the restriction? For discussion, see D. Terence Langendoen and Thomas G. Bever, "The Interaction of Speech Perception and Grammatical Structure in the Evolution of Language."

9. For many speakers of English, there is still a restricted set of syntactic environments in which the deletion of the relative pronoun standing for the subject of its own

clause is permitted. Examples of the sorts of sentences that such speakers find grammatical are the following:

337. I wonder who it was defined man as a rational animal.
338. There's someone downstairs wants to speak with the missus.
339. Here's a book will help you find happiness in life.

If you are such a person, characterize the class of sentences for which you permit the deletion (you may find that you use sentence types other than those given in 337–339).

†10. The relative pronoun or particle may not be deleted under any circumstances when the relative clause modifies an interrogative pronoun. Consider the following sentences:

340. Who who/that is in the room likes you?
341.*Who is in the room likes you?
342. Who likes you who/that is in the room?
343.*Who likes you is in the room?

The ungrammaticality of 341 follows directly from the perceptual strategy discussed in Section 2. That of 343 does not. Why not? Now consider:

344. Who whom/that you like is in the room?
345.*Who you like is in the room?
346. Who is in the room whom/that you like?
347. Who is in the room you like?

The ungrammaticality of 345, similarly, does not follow from the perceptual strategy. Why not? Notice, however, that the relative pronoun or particle may be deleted if the relative clause is extraposed, as in 347. This suggests the hypothesis that English grammar is set up so as to prevent occurrences of interrogative pronouns followed immediately by nominal expressions (other than relative pronouns). Notice that the automatic inversion of subject and auxiliary verb in questions in which the interrogative pronoun stands for the object accomplishes this same end:

348. Whom do you like?
349. *Whom you like?

Can you think of any reason why sequences of interrogative pronouns and nominal expressions are avoided in direct questions?

11. There is a type of relative clause in which the antecedent of the relative pronoun appears to be an entire sentence. Consider, for example:

350. My best friend was arrested yesterday, which upset me very much.
351. The unemployment rate dropped again last month, which the government finds encouraging.

Postulate deep structures for examples like these, and present arguments defending your analysis.

12. Why, in the sentence:

352. It's John who doesn't like pistachio ice cream.

does the relative clause *who doesn't like pistachio ice cream* not modify *John*? (Hint—notice that restrictive relative clauses usually are not permitted to modify proper nouns in English). For a suggestion on the deep-structure analysis of sentences of this sort (the so-called "cleft sentences"), see Section 15 of this chapter.

13. What is the antecedent for the relative pronoun in the following sentence?

353. If John likes parties, which he does, then he'll really enjoy the one we're throwing tonight.

Under what conditions can relative clauses such as *which he does* in 353 be formed?

14. The analysis of sentences like 39 as having deep struc-

tures like those of 41 receives support from grammaticality judgments like the following:

354. Anyone who knows Mary likes her.
355.*Anyone likes Mary.

Why?

Account for the ambiguity of the sentence:

356. If anyone can solve this problem, Tom certainly can.

15. Conditional sentences such as 41 seem, in general, to be paraphrasable by *either* . . . *or* sentences in which the first part of the conditional is made negative; thus 41 is paraphrasable as:

357. Either a person doesn't smoke or he stands a good chance of developing lung cancer.

Do you think therefore that 41 and 357 should be assigned the same deep structure? Why or why not?

16. Account for the ambiguity of:

358. My vegetarian aunt is coming to dinner.

17. Whiz deletion and adjective preposing are restricted in rather complicated ways in the presence of a negative element in the relative clause. On the basis of the following examples, and others you think of, formulate these restrictions as precisely as you can.

359. The administration only talks to students who are not troubled.
360.*The administration only talks to students not troubled.
361.*The administration only talks to not-troubled students.
362. The administration only talks to students who are not troubled about the draft.

363. The administration only talks to students not troubled about the draft.
364. The administration only talks to students who are not very troubled.
365.*The administration only talks to students not very troubled.
366. The administration only talks to not-very-troubled students.

18. Certain attributive adjectives do not originate as predicate adjectives in deep structure, as the following examples illustrate:

367. The former king of France is bald.
368.*The king of France who is former is bald.
369. The company does not hire notorious liars.
370. The company does not hire liars who are notorious.

(Even though example 370 is grammatical, its meaning is not that of the usual sense of 369.) What is the deep-structure origin of the attributive adjectives in 367 and 369?

19. Give a transformational account of the origin of the expressions *whoever* and *whatever* in sentences like:

371. Joan's father disapproved of whoever she brought home.
372. Whatever you want will be brought to you.

†20. Account for the ambiguity of the sentence:

373. What John disliked was being ignored by everyone.

21. Check the formulation of the relative-clause-formation transformation to see whether the sentence:

374. The witness, he testified already.

corresponds to an intermediate step in the derivation of the sentence:

375. The witness testified already.

from the underlying discourse:

376. Someone was the witness. He testified already.

Similarly, does:

377. A girl who became pregnant, my cousin married her.

correspond to an intermediate step in the derivation of 27 from 28? Note, however, that grammatically we do not obtain sentences like:

378.*My cousin, a girl who became pregnant, he married her.

22. In the sentence:

379. I found who John was looking for.

the clause *who John was looking for* has been reduced from *the one who John was looking for*, whereas in the sentence:

380. I wondered who John was looking for.

the same clause is an indirect question. Find sentences which are ambiguous in that the clause following the verb can be interpreted either as in indirect question or as a reduction of nominal expressions starting off as *the one who* or *that which*.

23. Although *whose* can function both as a relative pronoun and an interrogative pronoun, as in the sentences:

381. A man whose ideas I admire will speak tonight.
382. Whose ideas do you admire?

for many persons there is a condition under which *whose* can be used as a relative pronoun but not as an interrogative. What is that condition?

24. In interrogative sentences, the question-word is brought

to the front of the sentence. If the question-word is inside a larger nominal expression, the rest of the noun phrase may, and under certain circumstances must, be brought forward with it. What are the circumstances under which the entire larger nominal expression must be brought forward? Consider, for example, the following:

383. What did you see the top of?
384. Of what did you see the top?
385. The top of what did you see?
386.*Whose did you see head?
387. Whose head did you see?

25. Show that these same conditions hold for the bringing forward of relative pronouns in relative clauses.

26. Like interrogative sentences, exclamatory sentences such as:

388. What stories you tell!

may be embedded as content clauses in larger sentences, such as:

389. It amazes me what stories you tell.

Notice, also, that ambiguities between indirect questions and indirect exclamations are possible; consider:

390. I know what stories you tell.

Do these observations suggest a performative analysis of exclamations, such as 388?

27. It is said that the verb *beware* only occurs in imperative sentences such as:

391. Beware of Harry's ocelot.

since it cannot occur as the main verb of declarative or interrogative sentences, for example:

392.*John is bewaring of Harry's ocelot.
393.*Did John beware of Harry's ocelot?

Given the account of imperative sentences in the text, we should also expect that the verb *beware* can occur in object clauses of certain performative verbs. Does it, and if so, which ones?

28. It is known that young children have more difficulty in understanding passive sentences if, in the corresponding active ones, the same sorts of nominal expressions can be used as both subject and object. Thus, they have less difficulty in understanding a sentence such as:

394. The match was broken by the boy.

than:

395. The boy was hit by the girl.

since the sentence:

396. The match broke the boy.

is an unlikely one, whereas:

397. The boy hit the girl.

is perfectly normal. One might expect that the relative difficulty of understanding sentences like 395 would have its effects on the grammar of English, for example, in rendering certain passive sentences ungrammatical. Are there transitive verbs that do not occur or that rarely occur in the passive because of this difficulty?

29. Provide a syntactic account of what might be called the agentless construction in English, exemplified by sentences such as:

398. My psychology text reads like a novel.
399. Chihuahuas don't frighten easily.
400. John's old station wagon used to ride smoothly.

30. Give the affirmative counterpart to each of the following sentences:

401. No one saw anything.

402. No one saw something.
403. Someone didn't see anything.
404. Someone didn't see something.
405. Someone saw nothing.

31. In a familiar version of nonstandard English, instead of saying 161 or 162, one says:

406. John didn't see no one.

To describe this version of English, only a trivial modification in the rules of standard English syntax is required. What is it?

32. The standard dogma regarding "double negation" forbids the piling up of two or more occurrences of the sentence-negative element in the same simple clause. More than one negative in a sentence is permitted, however, if no more than one occurs in a single clause, as in the sentence:

407. No one denies that Jack doesn't love Jill.

There are, however, sentenecs that violate the dogma but that nevertheless have to be admitted as grammatical. Consider the child who, when asked if he wants mustard or relish on his hot dog, replies:

408. Well, I don't want no thing on it.

Also, consider a sentence such as:

409. At no time should there be no one in the room.

(The intended meaning of 409 is that someone should be in the room at all times.) How can the dogma be stated so as to permit sentences like 408 and 409 while still excluding those double-negatives that we agree are ungrammatical?

†33. Suppose we agree (following James D. McCawley in a

recent unpublished paper) that the deep structure underlying:

420. Max likes Brahms, but not Sid; he hates Brahms.

is the same as that underlying:

411. Max likes Brahms, but Sid doesn't like Brahms;
he hates Brahms.

Now consider:

412. Max doesn't like Brahms, but not Sid; he loves
Brahms.

Where does this leave us?

34. Consider the sentence:

413. I never thought you'd come.

This sentence appears to be ambiguous, paraphrasable
either as:

414. At no time did I think you'd come.

and as:

415. I thought you'd never come.

In order to obtain the latter interpretation, we would be
obliged to postulate a transformation that raises the negative element *never* (similarly, *not*) from the object clause
of *think* to a position immediately preceding the verb.
Are there other verbs that permit the raising of negative
elements in this way?

The rule, in any event, is subject to certain restrictions.
Note, for example, that it is inapplicable in case there
already is a negative element modifying *think*; a sentence such as:

416. I never thought you'd never come.

is unambiguous, and 416 is not paraphrasable as:

417. I never never thought you'd come.

35. Why, despite the surface structure similarity of the following sentences, are their deep structures quite different?

   418. Jones seems to antagonize people.
   419. Jones expects to antagonize people.

36. The restriction that the subject of the object clause of the verb *try* be coreferential with the subject of *try* is paralleled by a restriction on the reference of possessive modifiers of object nouns of the verb *try*. Thus:

   420. Luke tried his luck at blackjack.
   421.*Luke tried my luck at blackjack.
   422.*Luke tried Herb's luck at blackjack.

   Give other examples of this sort of restriction.

37. What transformations, and in what order, have applied in the derivation of the following sentence:

   423. We elected a man president who was unqualified for the post.

38. Is the extraposition transformation involved at all in the derivation of sentences such as:

   424. The hostess will see to it that everyone is comfortable.
   425. I'd appreciate it if you'd leave me alone for a few minutes.
   426. Everyone took it that George's candidacy was serious.
   427. I have it on good authority that there will be a fire drill tomorrow.

   If so, what is its effect?

39. According to Fillmore, a surface subject can originate inside of a nominal expression functioning in a particular role. Thus, we may assume that the verb *itch* occurs with only a locative role, as in the sentence:

   428. My foot itches.

However, the "possessor" of the itchy entity may be expressed optionally as subject, as in:

429. I itch on my foot.

Whether or not a possessor is extracted and made subject may condition the choice of verb, particularly *have* and *be*. Compare:

430. There was a party next door to us last night.
431. We had a party next door to us last night.

(Notice that the intended sense of 431 is not the one according to which we actually threw the party.) Give as careful an account of this phenomenon as you can, listing those verbs which, like *itch*, permit the extraction, and the conditions under which the extraction is allowed to take place.

†40. How can Postal's principle, which forbids the transformational crossing of coreferential nominal expressions, be used as an argument for the position taken, for example, by Chomsky in all his writings on the passive construction, that there is a passive transformation which actually interchanges the position of the agent (or instrument) and patient?

Notice also that while a sentence such as:

432. John pleased Harry.

is ambiguous, depending upon whether *John* is agent and *Harry* patient or *John* is stimulus and *Harry* patient, the sentence:

433. John pleased himself.

is only interpretable with *John* as agent and *himself* as patient. This can be accounted for on the basis of Postal's principle if we assume that when we are given the roles stimulus and patient, patient is made subject, stimulus is made object, and there is a later transformation that interchanges them.

BIBLIOGRAPHY

Bach, Emmon. *An Introduction to Transformational Grammars.* New York: Holt, Rinehart and Winston, 1964.

———. "Nouns and Noun Phrases." In Bach and Harms, eds., 1968, pp. 90–122.

Bach, Emmon, and Robert Harms, eds. *Universals in Linguistic Theory.* New York: Holt, Rinehart and Winston, 1968.

Bever, Thomas G., and William Weksel, eds. *The Structure and Psychology of Language.* New York: Holt, Rinehart and Winston, forthcoming.

Bloch, Bernard, and George L. Trager. *Outline of Linguistic Analysis.* Baltimore: Linguistic Society of America, 1942.

Bloomfield, Leonard. *Language.* New York: Holt, Rinehart and Winston, 1933.

Bolinger, Dwight. 1967. "Imperatives in English." In *Studies Presented to Roman Jakobson on the Occasion of His Seventieth Birthday.* The Hague: Mouton and Company, 1967, pp. 335–362.

Chomsky, Noam. *Syntactic Structures.* The Hague: Mouton and Company, 1957.

Chomsky, Noam. "On the Notion 'Rule of Grammar.'" In Fodor and Katz, eds., 1964, pp. 119–154.

———. "A Transformational Approach to Syntax." In Fodor and Katz, eds., 1964, pp. 211–245.

———. *Aspects of the Theory of Syntax.* Cambridge: The M.I.T. Press, 1965.

———. *Cartesian Linguistics.* New York: Harper & Row, Publishers, 1966.

———. "Remarks for Nominalization." In Jacobs and Rosenbaum, eds., forthcoming.

Chomsky, Noam, and Morris Halle. *The Sound Pattern of English.* New York: Harper & Row, Publishers, 1968.

Emig, J., J. Fleming, and H. Popp, eds. *Language and Learning.* New York: Harcourt, Brace & World, Inc., 1965.

Fillmore, Charles J. "The Case for Case." In Bach and Harms, eds., 1968, pp. 1–88.

———. "Lexical Entries for Verbs," *Foundations of Language* 4 (1968): 373–393.

———. "The Grammar of Hitting and Breaking." In Jacobs and Rosenbaum, eds., forthcoming.

———. "Review of E. Bendix, *Componential Analysis of General Vocabulary.*" *General Linguistics* 9 (1969): 41–65.

Fodor, Jerry A., and Jerrold J. Katz, eds. *The Structure of Language.* Englewood Cliffs, N.J.: Prentice-Hall, Inc., 1964.

Fraser, Bruce. "Some Remarks on the Verb-Particle Construction in English." In F. P. Dinneen, ed., *Monograph Series on Languages and Linguistics,* no. 19, Washington: Georgetown University Press, 1966, pp. 45–61.

Gleason, H. A., Jr. *Linguistics and English Grammar.* New York: Holt, Rinehart and Winston, 1965.

Gruber, Jeffrey. "Functions of the Lexicon in Formal Descriptive Grammars." Technical Memorandum of the Systems Development Corporation, Santa Monica, Calif., 1967.

Harris, Zellig S. "Cooccurrence and Transformation in Linguistic Analysis." In Fodor and Katz, eds., 1964, pp. 155–210.

———. "Transformational Theory," *Language* 41 (1965): 363–401.

Harms, Robert. *Introduction to Phonological Theory.* Englewood Cliffs, N.J.: Prentice-Hall, Inc., 1968.

Hasegawa, Kinsuke. "The Passive Construction in English," *Language* 44 (1968): 230–243.

Jacobs, Roderick, and Peter S. Rosenbaum, eds. *Readings in English Transformational Grammar*. Waltham, Mass.: Ginn-Blaisdell, forthcoming.

Jakobovits, Leon, and Murray S. Miron, eds. *Readings in the Psychology of Language*. Englewood Cliffs, N.J.: Prentice-Hall, Inc., 1967.

Jespersen, Otto. *A Modern English Grammar on Historical Principles*, vol. 3. Heidelberg: Carl Winters Universitätsbuchhandlung, 1927.

————. *Essentials of English Grammar*. New York: Holt, Rinehart and Winston, 1933. Reprinted, University: University of Alabama Press, 1964.

Katz, Jerrold J. *The Philosophy of Language*. New York: Harper & Row, Publishers, 1966.

————. "Recent Issues in Semantic Theory," *Foundations of Language* 3 (1967): 124–194.

————. *Semantic Theory*. New York: Harper & Row, Publishers, forthcoming.

Katz, Jerrold J., and Paul Postal. *An Integrated Theory of Linguistic Descriptions*, Cambridge: The M.I.T. Press, 1964.

Koutsoudas, Andreas. *Writing Transformational Grammars*. New York: McGraw-Hill, Inc., 1966.

Lakoff, George. *On the Nature of Syntactic Irregularity*. Cambridge: Harvard Computational Laboratory Report NSF–16, 1965. Forthcoming under the title *Irregularity in Syntax*. New York: Holt, Rinehart and Winston.

Langacker, Ronald. *Language and its Structure*. New York: Harcourt, Brace & World, Inc., 1968.

————. "Pronominalization and the Chain of Command." In Reibel and Schane, eds., 1969, pp. 160–186.

Langendoen, D. Terence. *The Study of Syntax*. New York: Holt, Rinehard and Winston, 1969.

————. "The Accessibility of Deep Structures." In Jacobs and Rosenbaum, eds., forthcoming.

————. "Formal Linguistic Theory and the Theory of Automata." In Bever and Weksel, eds., forthcoming.

Langendoen, D. Terence, and Thomas G. Bever. "The Interaction of Speech Perception and Grammatical Structure in the Evolution of Language." In R. P. Stockwell, ed., *Historical Linguistics in the Perspective of Transformational Theory*. Bloomington: Indiana University Press, forthcoming.

Lees, Robert B. *The Grammar of English Nominalizations.* Bloomington: Indiana University Press; The Hague: Mouton and Company, 1960.

Lees, Robert B., and Edward S. Klima. "Rules for English Pronominalization." In Reibel and Schane, eds., 1969, pp. 145–169.

Lenneberg, Eric. "A Biological Perspective of Language." In E. Lenneberg, ed., *New Directions in the Study of Language.* Cambridge: The M.I.T. Press, 1964.

———. *The Biological Foundations of Language.* New York: John Wiley & Sons, 1967.

Longacre, Robert. *Grammar Discovery Procedures.* The Hague: Mouton and Company, 1964.

Lyons, John. *Introduction to Theoretical Linguistics.* Cambridge and New York: Cambridge University Press, 1968.

Lyons, John, and R. J. Wales, eds. *Psycholinguistics Papers.* Edinburgh: University Press, 1966.

McCawley, James D. "Concerning the Base Component of a Transformational Grammar," *Foundations of Language* 4 (1968): 243–269.

———. "Review of T. Sebeok, ed., *Current Trends in Linguistics,* vol. 3." *Language* 44 (1968): 556–593.

———. "The Role of Semantics in Grammar." In Bach and Harms, eds., 1968, pp. 124–169.

———. "Where Do Noun Phrases Come From?" In Jacobs and Rosenbaum, eds., forthcoming.

Miller, George A. "Psycholinguistic Approaches to the Study of Communication." In D. L. Arm, ed., *Journeys in Science,* Albuquerque: University of New Mexico Press, 1967, pp. 22–73.

Miller, George, and S. Isard. "Free Recall of Self-embedded English Sentences," *Information and Control* 7 (1964): 292–303.

Perlmutter, David. "On the Article in English." In M. Bierwisch and K. Heidolph, eds., *Recent Advances in Linguistics,* The Hague: Mouton, forthcoming.

Peters, Stanley. "What Is Mathematical Linguistics?" In John Lyons, ed., *New Horizons in Linguistics.* Cambridge and New York: Cambridge University Press, forthcoming.

Postal, Paul. "Underlying and Superficial Linguistic Structure." In Emig, Fleming and Popp, eds., 1965, pp. 153–175.

———. "The Method of Universal Grammar." In P. Garvin, ed.,

The Place of Method in Linguistics. Bloomington: Indiana University Press, 1968.

Postal, Paul. "Problems in the Linguistic Representation of Reference." In Steinberg and Jakobovits, eds., forthcoming.

Postman, Neil, and Charles Weingartner. *Linguistics: A Revolution in Teaching.* New York: Dell Publishing Co., Inc., 1966.

Reibel, David A., and Sanford A. Schane, eds. *Modern Studies in English.* Englewood Cliffs, N. J.: Prentice-Hall, Inc., 1969.

Rosenbaum, Peter S. *The Grammar of English Predicate Complement Constructions.* Cambridge: The M.I.T. Press, 1967.

Rosenbaum, Peter S., and Roderick Jacobs. *English Transformational Grammar.* Waltham, Mass.: Ginn-Blaisdell, 1968.

Ross, John R. *Constraints on Variables in Syntax.* Dissertation, Massachusetts Institute of Technology, 1967.

———. "On the Cyclic Nature of English Pronominalization." In Reibel and Schane, eds., 1969, pp. 187–200.

Sapir, Edward. *Language.* New York: Harcourt, Brace & World, Inc., 1921.

Smith, Frank, and George A. Miller, eds. *The Genesis of Language.* Cambridge: The M.I.T. Press, 1966.

Steinberg, Danny, and Leon Jakobovits, eds. *Semantics: An Interdisciplinary Reader.* Cambridge and New York: Cambridge University Press, forthcoming.

Thomas, Owen. *Transformational Grammar and the Teacher of English.* New York: Holt, Rinehart and Winston, 1965.

Thorne, James L. "English Imperative Sentences," *Journal of Linguistics* 2 (1966): 69–79.

Vendler, Zeno. "Each and Every, Any and All." In *Linguistics and Philosophy,* Ithaca: Cornell University Press, 1967.

Weinreich, Uriel. "Explorations in Semantic Theory." In T. A. Sebeok, ed., *Current Trends in Linguistics,* Vol. 3, *Theoretical Foundations.* The Hague: Mouton and Company, 1966, pp. 395–477.

Whitney, William Dwight. *Essentials of English Grammar for the Use of Schools.* Boston: Ginn & Company, 1877.

INDEX

For the particular roles discussed in this book, see the entries under Agent, Cause, Content, Duration, Essive, Goal, Instrument, Location, Movement, Observation, Partitive, Patient, Result, Source, State, and Stimulus. For the particular transformations discussed, see the entries under Adjective preposing, Content-clause movement, Extraposition, Genitive formation, Imperative, Indefinite-pronoun replacement, Indirect-object movement, Infinitive formation, Interrogative, Negative, Negative raising, Object formation, Particle movement, Passive, Preposition deletion, Pronominalization, Reflexive-object deletion, Reflexivization, Relative-clause formation, Relative-clause movement, Relative-pronoun/particle deletion, Relative-pronoun-plus-*be* ("Whiz") deletion, Role deletion, Subject formation, Tense suffixation, *That* deletion, *To-be* deletion, and Topicalization.